Creating Confidence

THE SECRETS OF SELF-ESTEEM

Rex Johnson and David Swindley

ELEMENT

Shaftesbury, Dorset ● Rockport, Massachusetts
Brisbane, Queensland

© Rex Johnson and David Swindley 1994

First published in Great Britain in 1994 by
Element Books Ltd
Shaftesbury, Dorset

Published in the USA in 1994 by
Element, Inc.
42 Broadway, Rockport, MA 01966

Published in Australia in 1994 by
Element Books Ltd
for Jacaranda Wiley Ltd
33 Park Road, Milton, Brisbane, 4064

Cover design by Max Fairbrother
Design by Roger Lightfoot
Typeset by ROM-Data Corporation Limited, Falmouth, Cornwall
Printed and bound in Great Britain by Redwood Books Ltd,
Trowbridge, Wiltshire

British Library Cataloguing in Publication
data available

Library of Congress Cataloging in Publication
data available

ISBN 1-85230-577-0

Creating Confidence

Rex Johnson is a psychotherapist and holistic health practitioner with twenty years' experience of helping people with both personal development and physical health problems.

David Swindley is a psychotherapist and hypnotherapist, and the co-founder with Rex Johnson of the Dynamic Living Institute which runs courses in all areas of personal development for both private and corporate clients.

Contents

Acknowledgements

We would like to express our gratitude to Joanne Figov for contributing many hours of patient and thorough research, and to Colleen Johnson for her creative and painstaking editing.

Preface

This book is about self-esteem. Throughout his eighteen years in practice as a holistic healer, Rex has been convinced that people become ill because their lives aren't working, and the main reason why their lives are less fulfilling than they could be is because their self-esteem is poor. He has inspired many people to transform their self-images and in most cases they have gone on to live much healthier, happier and more successful lives.

Rex's approach is born out of hard experience. When he was a child, he had poor self-esteem and was lacking in self-confidence. He left school at the age of sixteen, the target of playground bullies, and took up karate. Drawing on his immense resources of discipline and perseverance, he gained two black belts and went on to teach many others.

After building up a successful business to pay his way through college, where he studied naturopathy, homoeopathy, osteopathy and medical herbalism, he established a large practice in his home city of Cape Town. Even so, he carried on studying until he was the most highly qualified practitioner in South Africa, using twelve natural therapies in a unique holistic health care system. His practice continued to expand, so he and his wife Colleen bought a large mansion and turned it into the biggest holistic healing centre in the country. Eventually, Rex realized he had progressed as far as he could in Cape Town. He wanted to help many more people than he was able to reach in South Africa, so he and his family moved to Bournemouth in Britain, where they settled down to rebuild their practice.

The tremendous upheaval in Rex's life caused by the complete change of environment, together with the challenge of starting up all over again, brought home to him the futility of relying on outside circumstances to bolster his self-confidence. *It dawned on him that the cause and cure lay entirely within himself*, and he began to study practical psychology seriously. The more he read, the more fascinated he became.

As he worked with his patients and continued his studies, Rex came to the conclusion that the root cause behind most illnesses is wrong thinking, which ruins not only someone's health, but his or her whole life as well. This led him to qualify in hypnotherapy and psychotherapy so that he could help his patients change their thinking patterns and their consciousness. He then combined his knowledge and his personal experience to develop the Dynamic Living Principles presented for the first time in this book.

However, he was acutely aware that, before going public, his most important task was to integrate the Principles into his own psyche. He duly set to work on himself, and soon the practice was thriving as never before. His whole life had turned around, becoming purposeful, fulfilling, challenging – and fun! He now has one big ambition: to help many others discover how to live happier, healthier and more successful lives.

He currently uses a total of fifteen therapies and regularly gives lectures and workshops covering all aspects of holistic health care and Dynamic Living. He has made numerous self-help tapes and, together with his partner David Swindley, is preparing several books.

Dave spent the first eleven years of his working life in business, serving some of Britain's best-known companies as a market researcher. He then decided to further his qualifications by studying for a Masters degree and subsequently went into education, keen to share his knowledge and experience. His interest in helping others to develop their potential was already well advanced before he became a university lecturer.

Although he was employed to teach a variety of business subjects, he applied his increasing awareness of personal development to his work, not always with the blessing of his employers! Many of his former students occupy senior positions in the business world, or have chosen to follow other varied and interesting directions: some have become authors, musicians and professional sportspeople, and others have set up their own businesses.

Like Rex, Dave didn't always enjoy a good self-image. He was uncertain of himself as a teenager, especially in social situations, but once he left home he realized that he wouldn't get very far unless he could overcome his shyness. In his early twenties he began focusing his mind on developing the qualities he wished to have.

Since then he has devoted twenty years to studying ways in which we can all live more happily, and has tried most of them out for himself. Starting with diet, exercise, self-hypnosis and meditation, he experimented with many natural health-care techniques, but he realized that it is not possible to enjoy good health and happiness unless your whole life is working for you and is purposeful and fulfilling.

During his eight successful years as a lecturer, consultant and writer he became increasingly disillusioned. He passionately believes that the purpose of education is to empower individuals to make the most of their lives. Frustrated with the system, he decided to become a psychotherapist and hypnotherapist, so he studied, qualified and set up his own practice. He also runs courses in business skills and self-management, and teaches and plays the piano.

We have applied our knowledge to our own lives, and are enjoying greater success than we could have ever imagined. We know our ideas work because we have seen them succeed in literally thousands of cases over the years. The Dynamic Living Institute, which we founded with Joanne Figov and Colleen Johnson, has one single purpose: to share our ideas with others so they, too, may benefit.

Naturally we have altered the names of the people whose inspiring stories we have included. Sometimes they would have been happy to reveal their true identities because they were proud of their achievements, but we thought it best to use pseudonyms to avoid causing embarrassment. You have our assurance, however, that every example is true.

We have avoided saying 'he or she' and 'himself or herself' or other such phrases denoting both sexes by using one or the other. Whenever this occurs we hope you will take it as read that we mean both. Our philosophy applies equally to men and women, young and old.

It takes twenty-eight days to change a habit – it doesn't matter whether the habit is a pattern of behaviour or a mental train of thought – and scattered throughout this book are ideas which build into a four-week programme. We have also produced two cassette tapes which will help you to harness the powerful forces of your unconscious mind in order to reach your goal. If you follow our suggestions for a minimum of twenty-eight days, you will literally be able to change your life by changing your mind.

There is an old saying, 'It doesn't matter if the signpost is rotten as long as it is pointing in the right direction.' We admit that occasionally we don't live up to our own expectations, but of one thing we are sure: read, understand and apply the ideas in this book and, to quote Thoreau, 'you will find success undreamt of in common hours.'

Rex Johnson and David Swindley

The Dynamic Living Principles

1. You create your own reality with your thoughts, feelings and attitudes.

2. You have the right to a better quality of life; to health, happiness and success.

3. The reason most people get ill is because their lives aren't working.

4. You can transform your life by changing your attitude.

5. Whatever your mind can conceive and believe, you can achieve.

6. Decide to build into yourself the qualities and characteristics you need for success.

7. You can have whatever you want in life, providing you are willing to invest the necessary time, energy and effort.

8. Live in the present moment. Life is a journey to be enjoyed, not a struggle to be endured.

9. Transform your conscious mind with the Dynamic Living Principles and your unconscious with the Dynamic Living Formula.

10. Allow yourself to be guided and supported by the Universal Intelligence which is within you and you will always be happy, healthy and successful and have the courage to follow your dreams.

1. You Can Only Rise As High As Your Self-Esteem

The Miracle Man

On 10 March 1981, Morris Goodman was flying his jet plane back from a pleasure trip when he crashed on landing. He was very severely injured; his top two cervical vertebrae were crushed. Doctors said he would have had no chance of surviving if he had crushed only one; two gave him less than no chance. He wasn't expected to make it through the night.

His kidneys, liver and bladder had ceased to function. He was reliant on a respirator because his diaphragm had stopped working. He couldn't swallow or speak since his throat muscles were no longer functioning. The doctors said he had no hope at all, but Goodman had other ideas; he was convinced he could make a full recovery. He managed to get his liver, kidneys and bladder working again. He somehow got his diaphragm to function so he could breathe. He used a ping-pong ball to exercise his throat so he could swallow and talk. After a few weeks he was discharged.

The consultant told him it was a miracle he had survived but unfortunately he would be paralysed for life and would never walk again. Morris Goodman smiled. 'Within a year,' he said, 'I'll walk back into your office and shake your hand.' The doctor shook his head in disbelief.

Within eight months, to the consultant's astonishment, Goodman walked back into the office and shook his hand. If he had believed the doctors he would have died, but he had tremendous courage and self-esteem and his belief in himself had seen him through. A film was made of his story, called *The Miracle Man*. If one man can achieve such a remarkable feat, why can't we all?

2 Creating Confidence

Self-Esteem Isn't Everything – Or Is It?

We have all come across people loaded with self-confidence and marvelled at their knack of getting on and living life to the full. Somehow, they seem able to take advantage of all the opportunities that come their way. So what is it that enables them to take the bull by the horns, time after time? What is this thing we call 'self-esteem'?

> *When you're as great as I am,*
> *it's hard to be humble.*
>
> Muhammad Ali

It is simply the feeling of worth you have about yourself: the value you place on *you*. Like oxygen or electricity, you can't see, hear, taste or smell it, but you know when it's not there. 'Self-esteem isn't everything,' said Gloria Steinem, 'it's just that there's nothing without it.'

High self-esteem is a feeling that you're worthy of all the good things in life, like happiness, good health, prosperity and fulfilling relationships. It is a positive feeling about yourself and an unshakeable belief that you can move in any direction you want and make a success of it. In contrast, low self-esteem is a sense of inadequacy and a belief you're not worthy of getting much out of life.

We see self-esteem as having two facets – your self-image and your self-confidence. When we discuss self-image, we mean how you see yourself; in other words, what you believe yourself to be. It is important to realize that it is not the image you try to put across to other people, nor is it necessarily the way you actually are. It is simply your perception of yourself, and it can either be accurate or quite misleading. We all know people who are talented, healthy and successful but still have a poor self-image. Self-confidence is your belief in your ability to accomplish.

You May Not Be What You Think You Are

Carl Rogers, the distinguished American psychologist, was careful to differentiate between the '*self*' and the '*self concept*'. It is an important distinction.

The 'self' is the real you, exactly as you really are. Rogers was convinced that everybody is innately positive, forward-looking, constructive, realistic and trustworthy, unless circumstances get in the way. This can happen, for instance, if a child is constantly criticized and begins to doubt herself through no fault of her own.

The 'self-concept' is the image you have of yourself, what you *believe* yourself to be. It develops over time and is heavily influenced by the way others treat you. The self-concept can, of course, be a complete misconception. Who would ever have imagined that John Lennon often asked the producer to disguise his voice using electronic effects? He had such a poor opinion of his singing that this is exactly what he did.

Self-Confidence Is What You Do

People with plenty of self-confidence believe they can do anything they choose and be competent at any activity they decide to pursue. Sometimes, a person can be fully confident in one area but completely lacking in another, like the scientist who is brilliant in his laboratory but fumbles hopelessly when asked to explain his findings to a seminar group, or the actress who stuns adoring audiences but avoids social situations because she doesn't believe she's good at talking to people. We have all seen very courageous sportsmen and women freezing when expected to give a speech in front of an audience at an awards ceremony on television.

We know from our own experiences that self-confidence can vary from place to place and hour to hour. You may be feeling perfectly happy and confident; somebody suddenly says something to upset you, doubts come flooding in and you feel shaken and unsure.

When Dave was a teenager, he was the sort of person you would always find in the kitchen at parties, too shy to talk to new people and too self-conscious to get up and dance. He would eat and drink until it was time to make an excuse and leave.

He was quite happy, however, doing things that would have terrified many enthusiastic party-goers. He had no butterflies when sitting exams, or playing the piano in front of an audience. Once, when at a young people's exhibition in London, he spotted a sign announcing a piano competition. He'd been rehearsing his favourite pop tune, so he decided to enter. Imagine his alarm when the person before him played that very piece! He had to play something he hadn't rehearsed, but to his amazement he won; and yet, in those days, he would have nightmares about going to a party. Clearly self-image and self-confidence are closely related. If you don't believe you are worthy of happiness and success you won't have the confidence to achieve it.

Let's take a look at an example of what can be achieved with the right attitude.

Mark is the buying controller of a huge retail company. At twenty-seven, he has a large staff, lives in an impressive house in the country with his wife and children, drives a prestigious car and travels all over the world.

You might think he was born with a silver spoon in his mouth, but it's not true. He was brought up in a deprived area of Liverpool and had to fight his way up life's ladder. He financed himself through university by running a second-hand car business and playing football for a semi-professional team. His parents didn't contribute to his education at all.

Yes, you may say, but he probably had one or two lucky breaks. Perhaps. But it's far from the whole story, because he created his own luck. At an early age, consciously or unconsciously, he decided to act confidently. He found that having confidence worked better for him than not having it, and by the time he reached his teens it had become a habit.

By utilizing the Dynamic Living approach, you can do it too! The decision to act confidently can be made at any stage of your life. It's never too early, or too late, to start.

Your Six Self-Images

You actually have six different self-images. You have a physical, an emotional, an intellectual and a social self-image. These are governed by how you see your physical appearance, your emotional state, your intellectual capabilities and your social attributes. You also have a 'real' self-image and an 'ideal', which are the way you actually see yourself, and how you would like to be.

Your Physical Self-Image

Everybody has definite opinions about their appearance; most of us could produce a list of our physical drawbacks quite easily. One person may think himself too tall or too short, too fat or too thin, too pale or too bald. Another may wish she had brown eyes instead of blue, bigger breasts, blonde hair instead of black, or a different shaped nose.

Some of these so-called faults are fairly easy to correct, and others can be changed with a little effort. You can wear high-heeled shoes to appear taller, colour your hair, or diet and work out at a gym if you want to lose weight. If the size and shape of your nose is important enough to you, you can have plastic surgery. If your self-image is affected by anything that can be changed, it is worth considering taking action; if not, you have to learn to make the best of what you've got. There is nothing you can do about the colour of your eyes, your height or the size of your feet. We all age, although some are uncomfortable with the idea and go to enormous and unnatural lengths to disguise it.

Sometimes others see these so-called defects as endearing, so learn to appreciate them. Wouldn't life be dull if we all looked the same? The fact is, your physical characteristics will only affect your self-image if you let them. We all know people who do not meet the supposed physical 'norms' yet are happy, attractive and popular, as Geoff's story shows.

Geoff was an overweight student who wore glasses and was already balding at the age of twenty. He was not particularly bright, but was always pleasant and outgoing, had a gentle wit and a reputation for helping others. He was never missing from student social functions, where his ungainly dancing was a source of amusement, and he could usually be persuaded to get up on the stage and tell a few jokes. He was popular with his male friends and never short of female company.

Our physical self-image is important and we have to do what we can to improve it, but ultimately we can't afford to let other people's derogatory comments carry any weight. We have to decide to be happy with ourselves.

Your Emotional Self-Image

Our feelings are a very important factor governing our emotional self-image. If we are positive, enthusiastic and happy, we feel good about ourselves. If we worry a lot, feel guilty and have frequent outbursts of anger and bad temper, we probably have a poor opinion of ourselves.

You can improve your emotional self-image by choosing positive emotions. This is not so difficult; think about it for a moment. Your feelings and emotions are governed by your thoughts. You choose your thoughts. It follows that you choose your emotional state by selecting which thoughts to hold in your head. This may sound strange at first, but it will become clearer to you as you read on. Choosing your thoughts is one of the most important steps along the road to high self-esteem.

Your Intellectual Self-Image

Your intellectual self-image was probably formed during your early days at school. You somehow knew whether your teacher liked you and thought of you as clever. You were aware that some children were able to grasp new ideas quicker than others. As you grew older, test results and examination grades were used as evidence that you were smart, average or slow.

If your teachers thought you were intelligent, you were encouraged to go to college and study for qualifications which could help your job prospects and improve your earning power for the rest of your life. If not, your formal education was brought prematurely to a close. This scenario is a tragedy, because the most important factor determining whether a child will do well at school is the expectation his parents and teachers have of him.

In one famous experiment, the names of two teachers were pulled out of a hat. They were told that they were the best teachers, judged by the results they had been getting, and that they would be given the brightest children in the school for a year to see how well they could perform. A year later, these children were getting the best grades not only in the school, but in the whole district.

Unknown to the teachers, the classes had been carefully matched so that they were roughly equal in ability and the teachers were selected at random, and were no more competent than their colleagues. The outstanding results were a result of nothing more than the expectations the teachers had of themselves and the children; expectations which had been created by the experimenters.

Most people are cleverer than they think they are, but can't bring themselves to believe it. Often their limiting belief can be traced back to childhood. Sadly, they don't attempt anything that requires too much intelligence because they have convinced themselves they can't do it.

Your Social Self-Image

This is what you *imagine* other people think of you. It is not usually what they *actually* think of you; many people suffer agonies thinking others have a poor opinion of them when it is not at all true.

Dave recently attended a course during which the students were asked to write what they thought of their colleagues and pass their comments anonymously on to each other. Everyone was amazed how well others regarded them!

It isn't surprising that we can often be mistaken about others' opinions of us. Very few of us take the time and trouble to express our feelings to each other. We feel awkward paying compliments, no matter how sincerely felt.

It's nice to be well thought of by your friends and colleagues, but in most cases how they see you is not the main issue. Others are much too busy worrying about themselves and what everybody else thinks of *them* to be concerned with you. If you allow yourself to be governed by what you imagine other people think, you won't get very far. It's your opinion of yourself that really matters.

Your 'Real' Self-Image Versus Your 'Ideal' Self-Image

Your *'real'* self-image is your view of yourself right now. It dictates your behaviour in every situation you face, determines how you relate to others, influences your success in your chosen career and the goals you set for yourself. Your feelings of worth and fulfilment are directly related to it.

Your *'ideal'* self-image is how you would like to be. Try this exercise: sit back, close your eyes and imagine what your life would be like if you suddenly had all the good qualities you've always wished for.

Do you, for instance, tend to put things off? Imagine the relief, the sense of accomplishment and freedom if you knew that all your present tasks were behind you, instead of looming like ominous dark clouds.

Are you untidy or disorganized? Pretend, for a moment, that you are a paragon of efficiency, and see the clutter around you restored to perfect order. Notice how it's suddenly easier to think straight? And what a delight to know where everything is!

How about your diet? If you think you eat too much junk food, picture your sylph-like figure and feel yourself bouncing with all the energy you would have if you could say 'no' to all that stodge.

Now – what are you going to do about it? Continue to indulge in wishful thinking? Forget all about it and stay as you are? You don't have to do either. There is a wise old saying 'If you can dream it you can do it.' Can you think of any good reason why you could not reach the highest levels of your personal best? Imagine the difference it would make to your life!

The truth is that you are never going to rise above the level of your self-esteem. If your self-esteem is low, you will find it impossible to get as much out of life as you should. Decide *now* that you are going to take the steps necessary to raise it. There is no reason on earth why you should live an unhappy and disappointing life.

Your Plan Of Action

A poor self-image reduces your power, like driving an expensive sports car without releasing the brakes, or owning a Ferrari fitted with a Mini engine. It inevitably leads to a lack of confidence, a feeling that whatever you do won't be good enough, or whatever you try you won't succeed. Make the decision to take your foot off the brake!

In your mind, formulate a definite idea of the person you would like to be – and start working towards it. Talk, act and think as if you are already that person. Use visualization, affirmations and all the other self-help techniques described in this book. After a while, your behaviour will start to change and, like a snowball rolling downhill, the transformation will gather momentum until your self-esteem blossoms and your life circumstances become everything you have ever wanted.

SUMMARY OF CHAPTER 1

1. Self-esteem is the feeling of worth you have about yourself. High self-esteem is a belief that you are worthy of all the good things in life.
2. Your self-image, or self-concept, is the way you see yourself. It is not necessarily how you actually are, or how you appear to others.

3. Self-confidence is your belief in your ability to achieve the things you want to. It is closely related to your self-image.
4. Most people are more confident in some situations than others. You can utilize the feelings of self-assurance you enjoy in one situation to give you a boost of confidence in another.
5. You are never going to rise above the level of your own self-esteem. Decide that you want it. Affirm that you will take action to improve it.

EXERCISE

1. Make sure you have half-an-hour to spare so you can sit quietly, undisturbed. Have a piece of paper and a pen to hand.

   Write down ten good points about yourself. Don't be afraid to be honest. Everyone has many positive qualities, so choosing just ten shouldn't be too difficult.

   Next, write ten negative points about yourself. Be as frank as you like. When you've made your list, go through each point in turn and ask yourself, 'Is this really true? Or is it just a belief I picked up which isn't really the way I am?'

   Which list was easier to compile? The ten good points, or the ten bad? Why do you think this is?

2. Go through your list of negative points. Cross out each word or phrase and write the exact opposite in its place. For example, if you wrote 'angry,' replace it with 'calm' or 'peaceful'. Replace 'lazy' with 'industrious'. Notice how you feel as you write.

3. Take each of your positive words and use them to complete the following sentence:

   I am . . . .

   Now, either (a) write out each sentence on a postcard, carry it around with you, and read it out loud or to yourself at regular intervals; or (b) record them onto a cassette tape. Listen frequently and repeat them to yourself as often as you can.

   These sentences are 'affirmations'. You will become more familiar with them in Chapter 11. They are a powerful tool for changing your perception of yourself.

2. You Can't Afford To Have Low Self-Esteem

Roland's mother and sister both died of cancer when he was in his early twenties. At first, he was devastated. He could have chosen to feel victimized by life's misfortunes, but he had a naturally positive outlook and a keen sense of adventure. He decided to quit his job as a secondary school teacher, which he wasn't enjoying, and travel round the world.

He set off with very little money and a small bag packed with a few personal belongings. For five years, he worked his way from country to country, earning money by playing the piano in bars and doing any work he could pick up until he'd been to so many countries it was easier to list those he hadn't visited than those he had! During that time he met hundreds of interesting people, had many exhilarating and exciting experiences (as well as several life-threatening ones) and is now settled in southern France, teaching, playing music and engaged to a local girl. He is truly living his dreams.

How did he do it? He's no more clever or talented than many hundreds of thousands of people. The difference boils down to nothing more than a decision he once made. He simply chose the direction he wished to pursue and went for it.

What's stopping you from doing what you would really like to do? Self-doubt? Not intelligent enough, gifted enough, well enough qualified? Just don't have what it takes? Actually, it's none of these things. It's your *belief* in them that's shackling you. Your attitude towards your own capabilities, your self-image, could be the only thing that is holding you back.

Everybody, including you, has the right to high self-esteem, but you have to apply yourself. Sometimes you can earn it by having a go at fulfilling a cherished ambition, and you might be pleasantly surprised at the 'lift' you get, but mostly you will have to take firm control over yourself and your life. You will have to work hard, discipline your thinking, break through 'failure' and have a certain amount of resilience to cope with the inevitable ups-and-downs.

It's a chicken-and-egg situation. Only when you feel good about yourself will you be in charge of your life, and only when you are in charge of your life will you feel good about yourself. The more self-assured you are, the greater will be your natural inclination to take control. But even when it seems you have a long way to go, you will always, if you dig deeply enough, find within you the strength and resources you need to make your dreams come true.

What do you notice about people who have a good opinion of themselves? Probably the first thing is their relationships with others. Self-confidence is like a springboard for getting on well with others and attracting the people we want into our lives. Without it, we are always slightly on the defensive, interpreting other people's comments and actions, however innocent, as veiled attacks.

Think of half-a-dozen or so couples you know. Rate each individual on a scale of one to ten, where 'ten' means he or she has high self-esteem and plenty of self-confidence, and 'one' means he or she has low self-esteem and no confidence at all. We would be very surprised if any couple differs by more than two points, because like tends to attract like; we want to be with someone with whom we feel compatible, and we don't feel comfortable with someone whose level of self-esteem is too dissimilar from our own. Romantic choices are closely connected to how you see yourself.

The second noticeable feature of a person with a good self-image is their willingness to have a go at anything that takes their fancy, to take risks that others would avoid and to experience life to the full. They are often to be found enjoying active sports, travelling to distant lands to experience different cultures, setting up their own businesses, and taking up interesting hobbies.

Perhaps less obvious is the connection between self-esteem and health. Over the years, we have noticed a strong correlation between a good self-image and good health, and inevitably, between a poor self-image and illness. Many people literally worry themselves sick. Confident, self-assured people have more peace of mind, more energy and better health.

Self-belief is essential to success in virtually everything you do. Your marriage, friendships, career, leisure pursuits and every endeavour you may contemplate will be more fulfilling if you feel good about yourself and are willing to 'have a go' without being frightened of failure.

Hidden Depths

Sometimes we are amazed to discover abilities and interests in others that we couldn't possibly have imagined from their behaviour. We might think that a colleague or neighbour is too shy to get up to anything adventurous, and be quite wrong. Still waters run deep!

On the other hand, it is a mistake to think that loud, arrogant people have high self-esteem and quiet people have not. Nothing could be further from the truth. Usually, the most confident people feel no need to shout about their achievements; they just get on with their lives, doing as they please and enjoying themselves.

Dave once worked with a young researcher who appeared timid and self-effacing. Her colleagues were astonished to find out, by accident, that she was one of Britain's leading rock climbers! And imagine the surprise among the neighbours when they discovered that Eric, an old-age pensioner who was seen every morning taking his dog for a walk in the local woods, was a highly decorated war hero.

Belinda was a secretary, approaching retirement, whose passion was cycle-touring. Every summer she and her pensioner husband would take off to an exotic country carrying heavy rucksacks on their backs and panniers on their bikes. Together, they had cycled and camped on every continent, had visited over thirty countries and had undergone hardships that would have challenged a Royal Marine.

We all know people like this. To get the most out of life, follow their example! Decide what you want to do and 'have a go'. Don't allow yourself to be put off by anything others may think or say. Believe that you *can* and you'll find that it's true. Every success, however small, will raise your self-esteem another notch.

> *Everyone has three characters – that which they exhibit, that which they have, and that which they think they have.*
>
> Alphonse Kan

A Poor Self-Image Can Ruin Your Life – But Only If You Let It

As a teenager, Dale was very unhappy. His parents didn't seem to appreciate him even though he did well at school. He found it hard to get on with his classmates and was convinced he was a failure at everything that mattered.

By the time he was eighteen, he was smoking forty cigarettes a day, too cowardly to take his own life but unable to face the thought of living. When he left home, he couldn't cope with his newly found freedom, discovered alcohol and drugs, and was frequently ill. His doctor put him on tranquillizers and sleeping pills. He became more and more reliant on them.

He was so shy, nobody noticed him – until he met Lara. She worked in the next office, and although she wasn't exactly his idea of a beauty queen and had a biting turn of phrase, he was flattered by her attentions. He couldn't remember any woman showing an interest in him before.

Although Lara was engaged to another man, Dale's relationship with her grew, and eventually she moved in with him. Now he was no longer alone, and he enjoyed having someone to talk to and to go out with. After a few months, Lara started pressing him to get married. The very thought of it appalled him; he didn't feel ready at all, and her sarcasm and aggressive behaviour were beginning to annoy him. He'd already lost several friends because of her vicious tongue.

One day, when Dale had had too much to drink at a party, Lara pounced. She announced that they were getting married later that year. Next morning, when Dale recovered from his drunken stupor, he was too timid and too hungover to argue with her.

During the weeks leading up to the wedding he became convinced that Lara wasn't right for him. Even his friends tried to talk him out of it. His father journeyed to see him to warn him he was making a great mistake, but he didn't have the courage to face her and back out even though he knew that his father was right. He was afraid of being alone again.

The marriage was, inevitably, a complete disaster. From the day they returned from their honeymoon, Dale became more and more unhappy. In time, they had two children and he grew to detest his wife; he would go out as much as possible and take his children away at weekends to avoid seeing her.

After seven years, Lara filed for divorce on the grounds that Dale wasn't spending enough time with her and was ignoring her wishes. He didn't know whether to laugh or cry. 'If she wants out,' he decided after battling with the dilemma for a long time, 'she should push off and leave the children with me.' Unfortunately, in the end the court gave him no choice. He was forced to move out, leaving his beloved children to the whims of their neurotic mother, and all his financial assets tied up in the house he was no longer allowed to enter without Lara's permission.

Hammered by regrets, loneliness and guilt, Dale's self-esteem hit rock-bottom. He was drinking heavily, staying up all night and turning up late for work. He was permanently drained, and his employers asked him to leave. He felt very sorry for himself.

Then, by chance, he saw a poster advertising a talk on hypnosis, and went along. The speaker was an internationally known writer and broadcaster, and Dale was fascinated. After the talk, he gathered his courage and asked the speaker if he could go and see him. That conversation changed his life.

Dale went for six hypnotherapy sessions interspersed with plenty of 'homework' which helped him turn his whole psyche around. He discovered self-hypnosis and visualized himself daily as a successful person. He carried a small card listing some affirmations which he constantly repeated to himself. He began to take care of his body; he became a vegetarian, took up running, and attended a gym three times a week. He read self-improvement books and listened to inspirational tapes.

In the next eighteen months, Dale's life improved dramatically. He met a lovely girl, who he married. He landed an excellent job, bought a large house in a pleasant seaside town and before long was the father of two more wonderful children. For the first time in his life, he was really happy. He had learnt how to create the circumstances he wanted.

Lara, however, was still lurking in the background, determined to sabotage his new-found happiness in every possible way. She attempted to prejudice Dale's two eldest children against him and his new wife. She criticized the whole family perpetually, taking pleasure in playing on any weaknesses she could find. She also did everything she could to ensure that both her children were spiteful towards their young half-brothers.

But Lara's plan backfired. Her machinations actually drew Dale's family closer together, and fostered greater understanding, warmth and tolerance, not only between Dale and his wife, but among the four children as well. As Dale's self-awareness grew, he saw clearly that all his problems were due to the low self-esteem he suffered as a young man.

He now knows he would never have allowed Lara to manipulate him if he had been more self-assured. Every attempt made by his ex-wife to cause friction only strengthens his determination to build up the self-esteem of his four children so they won't ever make the same mistakes he did.

Recognizing the Problem

Dale was able to recognize his self-image problem and do something about it, but many people never get that far. They know their lives aren't working as they should, but think it's because they aren't well enough qualified, or find some other excuse. They accept a poor self-image, believing it's something they acquired early in childhood **and that it can't be changed.**

One example is Tracy, a highly qualified nursing sister who didn't seem to be able to cope with pressure, and yet insisted on building up her portfolio of qualifications. She looked so stressed her colleagues were concerned for her health. She hadn't had a holiday in twenty years, preferring to stay at home and work. One day, she confided in a friend that she was studying for a Master of Arts degree and intended to follow it up immediately with a Doctorate. When asked why she insisted on pushing herself to the limit in this way, she replied that she felt so unworthy.

Someone with rock-bottom self-esteem like Tracy could collect five Doctorates and still be unhappy. She will always feel unworthy until she takes deliberate steps to improve her self-image. She's not unusual. Believing that you can change your perception of yourself is the first step to achieving it.

One of the difficulties is that low self-esteem breeds a lack of confidence which makes it even harder to climb out of the rut. We are full of excuses: 'I can't,' 'I have three children to support,' 'My husband wouldn't like it,' and so on. So we stay put. 'Better the devil you know,' goes the old saying. 'It's too risky,' adds our ever-chattering mind. 'Don't jump from the frying pan into the fire.'

What You See Isn't Always the Reality

It is possible to be very successful outwardly, while inwardly full of self-doubt and self-hate. Being seen to be successful doesn't always give a person a good self-image. Many top business executives confess to lacking confidence, and often very famous people are riddled with fear, guilt and feelings of unworthiness. Some take desperate measures to hide their true feelings from the public and themselves.

We all know of famous entertainers who couldn't handle

their success despite being adored by millions of devoted fans all over the world. Sadly, some of the best-loved rock stars, actors, actresses and comedians resort to drink and drugs and end their lives prematurely in pitiful circumstances. We once read of a major star whose self-esteem was so low that he spent the last few years of his life dependent on drugs obtained from his doctor, stuffing himself with junk food and reliant on minders to meet his everyday needs. Recently, the newspapers have reported widely admired public figures secretly suffering from, for instance, eating disorders, sexual dysfunctions and alcohol dependency – all associated with anxiety and low self-esteem.

These people certainly tasted material success before their lives fell apart, but can we really describe them as successful? They may have achieved fame and fortune, but other areas of their lives were a complete disaster. Most people with low self-esteem, of course, don't even get that far. Lack of confidence and self-belief is usually a recipe for mediocrity and unhappiness in all areas of our lives.

The Circle of Despair

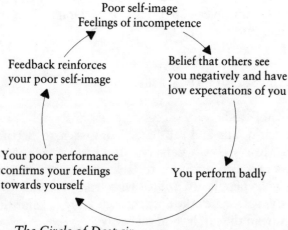

Figure 1. *The Circle of Despair*

A lack of confidence tends to produce destructive behaviour and stagnation. It's a self-perpetuating circle of despair. If you feel badly about yourself, you believe you can't accomplish anything worthwhile and that others have no faith in you either. So you perform badly and meet your own expectations, which reinforces your poor self-image.

You can reverse the Spiral by intervening at any point, applying Dynamic Living methods to reshape your thinking and actions. For instance, you could decide to do something really well, put everything you've got into it and enjoy the feelings of competence it brings. Then notice your self-image improving. Or you could use mental reconditioning to change your perception of yourself, raise your expectations and then see your performance improve.

Whatever point of entry you choose, apply the techniques described in this book consistently and you will succeed (see Chapter 8). Remember, there is no such thing as failure – only giving up too soon.

SUMMARY OF CHAPTER 2

1. High self-esteem has many benefits. It promotes good relationships, an adventurous outlook and good health. You feel happier and more in control of your life. It is probably the most important factor determining whether you make a success of your life or not. But it can't, by itself, guarantee success. All the qualifications, wealth and fame in the world can't compensate for a poor self-image. We can only say we are successful when every area of our lives is satisfying and well-balanced.
2. It is your right and your responsibility to work on your self-image, or you may become a burden to others instead of a joy to be with. You can find yourself making decisions you regret later, even if you know at the time that they are not right for you.
3. You don't have to be loud and arrogant to have a good self-image. Just go about your life with inner confidence, enjoying your sense of fulfilment.
4. Recognizing that you have a self-image problem and understanding it are the first steps to correcting it. Once you become aware

of the problems caused by a lack of self-esteem, you can judge whether your life choices are really your own or if they have been imposed by other people.

5. Dynamic Living methods break into the 'Spiral of Despair', that self-defeating circle which constantly reinforces itself, and reverse the process. There are many ways of leaving the Spiral – once you have decided that you want to!

EXERCISE

Complete the following sentences with six to ten endings each. Then look carefully at what you have written; it will help you to understand whether you have a self-image problem and where it lies.

1. It's not easy for me to be self-accepting when I . . . .
. . . .
. . . .

2. It's not easy for me to admit that . . . .
. . . .
. . . .

3. One of the things I like most about myself is . . . .
. . . .
. . . .

4. I like myself most when . . . .
. . . .
. . . .

5. There are some situations where I feel very good about myself, especially . . . .
. . . .
. . . .

6. One of the things I most dislike about myself is . . . .
. . . .
. . . .

7. I dislike myself most when . . . .
. . . .
. . . .

3. Sixteen Give-Aways Of A Poor Self-Image

Sadly, many people just don't have the confidence to try to escape from the unsatisfying, sad and hollow lives brought on by their lack of self-esteem. Think of all that needless unhappiness, that waste of human potential. Some readily admit that they aren't very self-assured, others even boast about it. Many desperately try to cover it up, but a well-tuned observer can spot the truth quite easily. Here are some clues.

1. The Critic

We all know people who are always criticizing themselves and others. Often they have done very little with their own lives and take perverse pleasure in belittling people who have been more successful. They are especially quick to condemn anyone who is different – different hairstyles, clothes, age, gender, race – the list is endless.

Some people can only get their kicks by attacking others or their property. They find it very easy to run down the efforts of other people, but are unable to come up with any constructive suggestions or take any positive action of their own. What an unhappy way of trying to justify themselves!

2. The Shrinking Violet

These people would do anything to avoid the limelight. They would rather shrink into the background, convinced that they're not worth anyone's attention. Try paying a shrinking violet a compliment. Instead of simply saying, 'Thank you, it's kind of you to mention it,' the chances are he'll say, 'It was nothing special,' or 'Somebody else would have done it much better.' People with a poor self-image cannot accept a compliment because they've spent many years behaving as if they are inadequate.

> *A modest man is usually admired –*
> *if people ever hear of him.*
>
> Edgar W. Howe

3. The Complainer

Some people take pleasure in complaining. If the weather is dull, they complain it's too cold; if it's sunny, it's unbearably hot. Whatever happens, they're not happy.

Sometimes, of course, there's good reason to complain. If you've had poor service, or bought something that wasn't up to scratch, it's only right that you should. It's important to distinguish between someone who has no difficulty asserting himself when he's been treated badly – who actually has good self-esteem – and someone who complains for the sake of it.

The difference is that complainers can't stop themselves complaining, get great pleasure from it, and take every opportunity to practise their art. The habitual moaner is wearing his poor self-image on his sleeve.

4. The Addict

Eating disorders, phobias and addictive habits such as anorexia, bulimia, smoking and alcoholism are usually giveaways that a person has low self-esteem. Most psychotherapists realize that the habit will melt away once the sufferer's self-confidence has been restored; his energies can then find more constructive outlets.

5. The Mouse

People with low self-esteem are afraid to reveal their true feelings because they cannot face possible rejection. They creep around like mice, too timid to express an opinion. They avoid complaining about goods and services even when they have every reason. They won't ever say 'No', even if they want to. They will never ask for a date even if they're besotted with the other person, or go and see the boss if they feel unfairly treated. They are too scared because they just don't think they're worth it.

Unassertive people are usually very reticent in company because they're worried that if they open their mouths they will embarrass themselves. Their motto is, 'Better to keep quiet and be thought a fool than speak out and prove it!' Of course, this is a harmful and limiting thought because they could well have something of value to contribute – but by keeping quiet no one will ever find out.

6. The Sheep

We live in a fashion-conscious society where value is placed on following the herd. It is the key to being accepted into certain circles. Sheep believe that the only way anyone is ever going to like them is to blindly follow the latest trend, whatever that may be. They are found in all age groups, but are especially common among teenagers and the young. They don't trust their own individuality enough to go their own way.

7. The Big Mouth

On the face of it, the big mouth is the opposite of the mouse. These people cannot stop talking, and come in two categories. The first is worried that he won't get another chance to say his piece; once he engages you in conversation it is hard to get away.

The second is an inveterate braggart, with scant regard for the truth. Lucy was such a person. Her life seemed to be going nowhere; she had no money, and no prospects because she lacked the necessary qualifications. She attempted to compensate for her situation by making promises to her eleven-year-old daughter and boasting loudly about all the things she was going to do one day, none of which ever materialized.

In five years, she had promised her daughter a pony, a cottage in Wales where they would breed horses, and a holiday in Australia. Then she said they would emigrate there and buy a large house with a garden. Recently, she announced that she was buying a barge that they could use for long holidays.

Needless to say, her daughter no longer believed a word she said; she'd had too many disappointments to be taken in again. Sadly, Lucy has lost the respect and perhaps even the love of her daughter through her own inadequacies, and has damaged her daughter's self-esteem as well.

A confident person has no need to boast, nor is she afraid to talk honestly about her successes. She is not afraid to say 'No' when she feels that she can't deliver a promise. A big mouth, on the other hand, has something to hide and will almost certainly let you down.

8. The Put-Down Expert

We once knew a woman who bragged about her ability to put people in their place. She had a quick insult, a barbed comment for everybody who crossed her path. She thought the only way she could impress was by using her caustic wit to put others down. Sadly she never noticed that the effect was exactly the opposite until she entered therapy; only then did she realize that she was putting her poor self-image on display and that she would have to change her behaviour.

9. The Begrudger

The begrudger is the jealous individual who feels that anyone who has something *he* wants doesn't really deserve it. This envy also extends to relationships; the jealous lover is so afraid that her partner will be unfaithful that she begrudges him going out alone in case he does something she doesn't approve of. What she is really saying is 'I don't understand how he could love me because I am so unworthy and he could easily find someone better.'

We know of someone who has won a recording contract with a large record company. Since his success, many of his former 'friends' have stopped associating with him. People who become successful are often disliked through jealousy, even by their close friends. They don't have sufficient self-confidence to be able to say 'Well done, I'm pleased for you,' and mean it.

10. The Blamer

The blamer is always looking for scapegoats. If something goes wrong, it's somebody else's fault. If his team loses, the referee's to blame. If he knocks something over and breaks it, it's not because of his clumsiness, but the thoughtlessness of the person who left it there in the first place. He may know deep down that he is to blame, but doesn't have sufficiently high self-esteem to acknowledge responsibility for his own actions.

11. The Comedian

People who have a sharp wit and a ready quip for every situation, no matter how serious, are often trying to cover up a self-image problem. They don't feel they will get attention unless they turn everything into a joke.

We're not saying that everybody who makes you laugh has a self-image problem. But we know many people who are frightened to say what they really feel because they don't think their contribution deserves to be taken seriously, so they make a joke out of the situation. After a while it can wear a bit thin, and others become irritated. The comedian just doesn't know when to stop.

12. The Shirker

People who shirk responsibility often reveal a poor self-image. They can easily be spotted in a work situation, especially if they've just been promoted. One person will throw his weight around arrogantly, treading on other people's toes and refusing to listen to advice or ask for any when decisions have to be taken. Another will carry on as if nothing has changed, treating his colleagues as if he is still one of the gang.

Self-assured people are quietly confident that they can handle the job, have no qualms about asking for help when they need it, and do not shirk the responsibility for making decisions and exercising control over their subordinates.

13. The Gossip

Gossips fear that they have nothing of interest to say, so they indulge in an orgy of sensationalism, hoping to attract approval and attention. One example is Pat, who is the office gossip. She craves attention and wants to be one of the 'in-crowd' but the only way she thinks she can get herself accepted is by spreading doom and gloom, scandal and rumour. She's so busy poking her nose into other people's business she hasn't realized that her workmates avoid her because they find her company too depressing.

Unfortunately, gossiping rarely achieves the desired results. Gossips are easily recognized for what they are and best left to their own devices.

14. The Walking Wardrobe

The way people dress says a lot about their self-image. Some either deliberately or unconsciously dress down as if they don't want to draw attention to themselves. Others do the exact opposite; they attire themselves in expensive designer wear with all the trimmings, or sport outrageous clothes which have the desired effect – they attract attention.

Anyone who has to use clothes in this way is really saying, 'I don't feel confident that people will like me for what I really am.' It's what's inside you, and what you make of it, that counts.

15. The Apologetic

A young student, Kathy, would preface every remark with the words, 'I'm sorry'. She would gingerly stick her head round the door and whisper, 'I'm sorry, it's only me,' or apologize for speaking up in class, afraid that she'd made a fool of herself.

If only she'd realized that she had nothing at all to apologize for! She was among the brightest students, worked hard and achieved good results. Her contributions were always telling. Her self-effacing attitude is a typical reaction to an unconscious feeling of unworthiness.

16. The First to the Bar

Very often the person who can least afford it is first to the bar, ordering the drinks. He believes he must buy his friendships because he won't be accepted on his own merits.

This manifests itself in other ways too. Children who are always lending their toys in an effort to make friends, workmates who offer others lifts and never accept one themselves, and teenagers who indiscriminately let everyone borrow their records, are all behaving in exactly the same way.

Their self-image problem will only be resolved when they

realize that their friends accept them for who they are, and that they don't have to pay for everything in order to be liked.

Change Your Behaviour and Your Attitude Will Follow

So there you have it: sixteen types of people who have a problem. Do you recognize any of them? If you know deep down that one or more of them applies to you, first admit it honestly to yourself and then set to work and turn things around.

We hope we have convinced you that your attitudes strongly influence your actions. It may surprise you to learn that it also works in reverse – what you do influences your attitudes. If you are aware that you're doing something which reflects a poor self-image, changing your behaviour will, in time, bring about a change of attitude.

Improving your self-esteem is all about taking small steps every day, consistently and with determination until your confidence improves. You will find that it gets easier as you go on. It's like adding drops of white paint to a tin of black paint. The change in colour will be negligible at first, but after a while the paint will turn dark grey, then light grey, and eventually, if you keep at it long enough, it will become white.

SUMMARY OF CHAPTER 3

1. People resort to many different behaviour patterns to hide a lack of self-esteem. We've listed sixteen of the most common, but there are literally hundreds.
2. If any of these apply to you, resolve to stop yourself from doing it. It will help if you use affirmations and visualization when you are in the relaxed 'Alpha' state described in Chapter 8. It won't necessarily be easy at first, but it will improve with practice. If you change the behaviour, your attitude towards yourself will start to improve.

EXERCISE

Go through the sixteen signs of a poor self-image and think of people you know who fit each description. What is it about their behaviour which gives the game away?

Can you add any more traits to the list? Perhaps you know someone with a poor self-image who shows it in a way we haven't mentioned.

Now for the $64,000 question. Which of these apply to you? Resolve now to eliminate these behaviours from your life. Make a list of anything you must stop doing. Write next to each item all the new behaviours you must adopt. Display your list in a prominent place. Every time you find yourself resorting to your old, unwanted behaviour, stop yourself and substitute the new.

Every time you succeed, reward yourself. Enjoy the feeling of achievement each small victory brings.

4. You *Can* Make That Change

Anthea was a social worker and the co-ordinator of child care services in a large city. She'd always had an ambition to travel but couldn't imagine how she could afford it on her salary. One day, a leaflet landed on her desk about a conference many thousands of miles away in Australia. She was about to file it in the waste bin when the doctor in charge walked in.

'What's that?' he asked.

'It's about a conference on children's issues in Australia in a few months' time.'

'Are you going?'

'Oh no,' she replied, 'I'd have to present a paper and I couldn't possibly do that.'

'Of course not,' said the doctor, 'you couldn't possibly do it.' Then he left the office.

Anthea sat at her desk feeling shaken, and fighting a rising sense of indignation. She went to the staff room for a cup of coffee, still holding the leaflet, and some colleagues were highly amused that she should even think about going. At last she couldn't contain herself any longer and went to see the doctor. She asked him what he'd meant by his remark, and he told her that if she had the attitude that she wasn't good enough and couldn't do it, then obviously she couldn't.

She asked what he thought, and his reply came like a bolt from the blue. 'Anthea, you can do anything you set your mind to and you can have anything you want, as long as you believe you can and put in the necessary effort.'

Spurred into action, she raised the £3,000 fare for the trip and worked very hard on the paper. The conference was a great success, her contribution was very well received and she enjoyed every minute of it.

If it hadn't been for the doctor's encouraging remarks about having confidence, the leaflet would have been thrown away! The decision to take that very first step resulted in a train of events which culminated in the achievement of her dream.

Making That Decision

There is an ancient Chinese proverb, 'The journey of a thousand miles begins with a single step.' So does the process of change. It really doesn't matter how far you feel you have to go, or how quickly you can progress, as long as you realize you can do it and keep going in the right direction. Don't think about the 'thousand miles' ahead; just focus on the short distance you need to travel today.

It is your right and your responsibility to have a good self-image. You owe it to yourself and to all those people you care about and who are close to you, especially your children. Although they cannot physically inherit high self-esteem, any more than *you* could, don't ever forget that you are helping to shape their lives; you are their role model and can help them make the decision to have a good self-image for themselves by following your example.

But the decision to have a good self-image can also be made later in life; we have seen dramatic changes in the lives of many of our clients and students. Many thousands of people have had a sudden realization that their lives are not working and something needs to be done. Sometimes, the clarity of insight is so powerful that change is instantaneous. Usually, though, it doesn't happen overnight.

> *We have to learn to be our own best
> friends because we fall too easily into
> the trap of being our own worst
> enemies.*
>
> Roderick Thorp

Rex firmly believes that it is impossible to be totally healthy unless you think well of yourself. One of his most successful patients was Esther, a lady in her forties who was suffering from psoriasis (an unpleasant skin condition), asthma and nervous disorders. At first, she could hardly breathe and walked hesitantly, and she regarded herself as a total failure. In time, Rex was able to treat her physical condition successfully using his holistic methods and counselling. With his encouragement she began to take short walks, then longer ones, and then she took up jogging, initially for ten minutes at a time, then longer. She enjoyed it so much she joined an athletics club and started running several miles a day. Then she entered half-marathons, marathons and eventually ultra-marathons. Even though she is not fast, she always completes the distance and last year was awarded the club's shield for the most consistent performer.

Chris was also convinced he was one of life's failures. He was suffering from depression and paranoia and was close to a nervous breakdown. He would sit up all night pulling the bristles out of a broom, and spent hours polishing his vast record collection. He had broken up with his girlfriend, hated his job and was convinced he had no future. As he progressed with counselling, his self-image began to improve and he slowly but steadily built up his self-confidence. He left his job to start his own business, which grew rapidly and was later sold when he was offered an executive position in a major company. Chris is now in his mid-thirties, happily married with a young son, exercises vigorously every day and exudes confidence.

Over the years, Dave taught many students who at first doubted their own ability but made tremendous progress and eventually graduated with good qualifications.

Ruth, for instance, was shy and lacking in intellectual self-esteem at first, but gained a first-class honours degree at the end of four years in which she worked hard to develop her self-confidence. Her final year dissertation was so good it was later published in a leading international academic journal, a very rare feat for a student's work.

Another shy eighteen-year-old, Jenny, admitted to a lecturer on her first day at college that she couldn't understand how she'd got on the course because the others seemed so much brighter than she. Nevertheless, she applied herself to her work and her confidence grew as each month went by. Like Ruth, she eventually gained a good degree and is now a senior executive with a credit card company.

So take heart! Anthea, Esther, Chris, Ruth and Jenny are ordinary people who transformed their lives by applying a few basic principles. As they tasted success, which increased as they persevered, their self-confidence improved remarkably. You can do it too, if you make the effort. Look again at Dynamic Living Principle number 7!

An Hour a Day

If someone told you that you could transform your life by devoting one hour a day to yourself, wouldn't you think it was worth the investment? Of course you would. And that's all it takes. An hour a day reading a self-improvement book, listening to inspiring tapes, using relaxation to change your conscious and unconscious thinking patterns, and practising the exercises in this book.

But a word of warning: we'll give you dozens of vital tips and ideas, but they will only work once you have taken the *decision* to take action for yourself and *follow it through*. Reading a book or attending a talk can leave you with a warm, satisfying feeling, but only application and persistence can bring results. Otherwise it is rather like expecting to get better just by reading the directions on a bottle of medicine rather than taking it.

We think it is vital, first of all, to understand how your self-image was formed. Then you can start to unravel the knots that tie you down. Your self-image began to develop early in childhood and was reinforced as you grew older by the way you saw your life experiences; your successes and failures, and other people's reactions towards you. The most crucial step of all is to realize that **a good self-image and therefore self-confidence is not something you can be given as a gift or receive in your genes. It is something you decide to have.** If you speak and act in a confident way, you will *be* confident.

When a young man enlists in the army, he is made from day one to conduct himself like a soldier so that he will become one. Similarly, if you *decide* to be confident and act confidently you will *become* confident. This may sound a tall order at first, but don't worry; it does get easier. Follow the Dynamic Living Principles and techniques revealed in the following chapters and you will see your self-image steadily improve until you are ready to take on the world!

SUMMARY OF CHAPTER 4

1. Change *is* possible; thousands of people have accomplished it. The methods we recommend have been used successfully with hundreds of people over a twenty-year period.
2. It is your right to have high self-esteem. If your self-esteem is low, it is your duty to work at it. A good self-image is something you decide to have. If you choose a good self-image and decide to be confident and act confidently, you will become confident.
3. If you spend an hour a day on yourself, you will make rapid progress. Read self-improvement books, listen to inspiring and relaxation tapes and practise the exercises in this book.

EXERCISES

1. Complete the following sentence. List at least six different endings:

   If I had a good self-image and plenty of self-confidence, I would

   . . . .
   . . . .
   . . . .

2. Make yourself very comfortable, either sitting or lying down. Close your eyes, take three very deep breaths and allow your imagination to flow freely.

Imagine that you have a wonderful self-image and loads of confidence. What would you do? How would you earn your living? How would you spend your spare time? Who would you be with? What other changes would you make in your life?

Let your mind drift for a few minutes, then open your eyes and write down everything you have thought of. Keep this list. You will have the opportunity to achieve all these things one day. Believe it and you can do it!

5. The Child Within

Martyn was relaxing in his armchair, reading his newspaper and enjoying a glass of beer when his three-year-old son, Jamie, ran in, excited to see his Dad at the end of another working day. As Jamie leapt up onto his father's knee, smiling broadly, calling 'Daddy, Daddy,' with his little arms outstretched, he accidentally knocked the beer over.

'You stupid boy!,' roared his Dad. 'You clumsy idiot. Can't you be more careful!' The last phrase was accompanied by several sharp blows to the head. He threw the boy onto the floor and dashed into the kitchen to get a cloth. Jamie was sent to his bedroom and went to sleep still sobbing.

Later that evening Martyn was getting another bottle of beer out of the fridge when it slipped from his hand and smashed on the floor. Needless to say, no one bellowed at him or cuffed him about the head. It was just an accident and accidents can happen . . .

Jamie's experience is not uncommon. It's possible something similar happened to you, not once, but many times when you were little. Each incident left its mark and compounded the one before.

The source of a poor self-image and lack of self-confidence is usually rooted in the feelings we had towards ourselves when small. Our parents, teachers, brothers, sisters, grandparents, aunts, uncles and friends all played their part. Furthermore, you can't avoid contributing to the self-esteem of your children.

Low self-esteem is one of the most serious problems in society. If it were a physical illness, it would be treated as an epidemic. So what is it about capable, sane individuals that makes them vulnerable to irrational doubts about their worth?

Understanding this is the first step to correcting the situation.

There is a story about a traveller who is lost in the country when he spots an old farmer sitting on a gate by the side of the road. He stops to ask him the way. 'I know exactly where you want to be,' replies the farmer, 'but if I were you I wouldn't have started from here.'

Like the traveller, we have no choice where we start from; at the present moment we are where we are, and no amount of wishing can make it otherwise. But it is useful to know how we got here since we might have to retrace our steps, find out where we went wrong and then change direction.

> *Character building begins in our*
> *infancy and continues until death.*
>
> Eleanor Roosevelt

From Babies . . .

A new-born baby has no self-image problem. It has no doubt it is the most important being in the universe. It has no hesitation in keeping the whole household up all night if it wants to.

As a baby, you craved attention and made your feelings perfectly clear if you felt neglected. For the first few months, all you had to do was yell if you needed anything, and someone came running to attend to you. You thought that all adults were there for your benefit and expected them to respond every time you made a noise.

As well as having your physical needs met, you hungered for love and acceptance and you could sense whether or not it was forthcoming. Love is not just a nice little extra for a baby, it is a matter of life and death. In a never-to-be-repeated experiment many years ago, scientists in a hospital selected two groups of new-born babies. Both groups were given everything they needed physically – food, warmth, clean clothing and so on – but one group had frequent cuddles and lots of attention, and the other did not. After a short while babies in the second group started to become ill and die. Alarmed doctors quickly aborted the exercise.

You instinctively knew whether you were wanted and loved or not without your parents having to say or do anything. You could sense how they were feeling towards you, and for some the seeds of a poor self-image are sown even at this tender age. Fortunately, most tiny babies are showered with affection and attention by their parents.

. . . To Toddlers . . .

However, it began to change once you became mobile. All of a sudden you were prevented from doing some of the things you wanted to. Those big people around you would occasionally get angry when you crawled where you shouldn't, or threw your food on the floor. You were dumped in a playpen to keep you out of trouble, strapped into your pushchair and made to wear reins to stop you wandering where you chose. Naturally these restrictions were not to your liking and took some getting used to.

You could still remember when all you had to do was squeak and an adult appeared instantly, but by now that service was deteriorating. You often had to wait before your demands were satisfied, and you had to learn to conform to the wishes of others. Your self-esteem had begun to be shaped by the world around you.

At times, you made it hard for your parents to love you. As a baby, you had deprived them of sleep and prevented them from doing as they chose. Now, as a toddler, you broke things, threw your food on the floor and squabbled with your brothers and sisters. After a while, your parents stopped thinking this was cute.

You learnt to understand speech and to communicate using language, and began to realize that your behaviour was not always approved of. When your parents considered you naughty or rude, they told you so. Occasionally you were shouted at, even punished by having privileges withdrawn or being smacked. Sometimes you were told off for doing something you didn't think was wrong, making you feel confused and unhappy.

This is actually quite unfair. Naughtiness is a deliberate decision to do something you know you shouldn't, but a very young child has no concept of 'what it shouldn't do'. So every time you were told off for being naughty, your feeling of acceptance and belonging diminished still further.

Attractive children are luckier than most. They soon realize they can use their appearance to win favours from adults. The beautiful, fair-haired little girl is constantly reminded, even by complete strangers, that she's cute. The scruffy, shabbily dressed child is shunned through no fault of his own. He didn't decide his own features, and can't help how he is dressed, but he senses that he's not valued as much as the well turned-out child who has been taught good manners.

One of the most traumatic experiences you faced was starting school. You went from being at the centre of your parents' lives to being just one of a large group of children who were expected to conform to a strange set of rules. Your teachers wanted you to be happy and to do well at your lessons, but with thirty other children in the class, maintaining discipline was their top priority.

Even a child's performance at school is linked to appearance. Teachers simply do not expect beautiful children to be dull, and experiments have shown how teachers' expectations of a child influence his success.

What happens, then, to the 70–80 per cent of children who do not find themselves winning the 'good looks' stakes? They soon begin to feel less worthy than the others. They notice other children receiving more attention, and as they grow up, quite innocent remarks reinforce their negative feelings because they have learnt to interpret them as criticism.

> *Work hard to create in your children a good*
> *self-image. It's the most important thing you*
> *can do to ensure their success.*
>
> H. Jackson Brown, Jnr

...To Juniors...

Research has shown that we received 25,000 hours of parental input by the age of twelve, most of it disapproving. By the time we left home, we had been criticized, told off or punished at least 70,000 times. For every word of praise, encouragement or trust we received ten negative injunctions.

We wanted the opportunity to try new things, to help Mum and Dad, to make things, yet how often were we told, 'Let Dad do it,' even when we knew we were quite capable of doing it ourselves. Every such incident dented our confidence and lowered our feelings of competence.

> *Never help a child with a task at*
> *which he feels he can succeed.*
>
> Maria Montessori

Most parents wanted to teach us what they thought we needed to know, but used methods which left much to be desired. When we did something good, often they didn't even notice. They were frequently dismissive or sparing in their praise. When we did something bad, we were rebuked: 'You naughty child, you horrible little boy, you wicked girl!' By the age of seven, we were quite capable of knowing when we deserved to be censured and when we did not. We felt rejected, angry, puzzled, betrayed.

When we were young, most of us were in the care of adults who loved us, but who either didn't know how to express their love or were too busy to take the time to tell us. Frequently when we wanted someone to play with us or give us their attention we were told 'I'm busy,' or 'I don't have time.' The message was clear; 'What I'm doing is more important. I have greater priorities than playing with you.'

When Samuel Johnson was a young man, he was asked what was his happiest childhood memory. 'I remember the day my father took me fishing,' he said. 'The two of us spent a whole day together.'

His father had kept a diary, and years later, when he died, someone looked up the entry for that day. 'Took Samuel fishing,' it said, 'another wasted day.'

We knew that parents were supposed to love their children, so we trusted them. We wanted them to notice us, and nothing pleased us more than individual attention from them. It made us feel wanted and special, and if they didn't make time to spend with us, we assumed it was our fault because we were unworthy in some way.

A child who feels starved of affection and approval will try to win them by conforming to her parents' expectations. She will obey in order to avoid losing her feeling of 'belongingness'. If they express their approval of her, she begins to develop a sense of competence and worth. 'I'm a good girl,' she thinks, 'I'm alright as I am.'

She learns to stay out of trouble by doing as she's told and submitting to her parents' way of thinking. The rights and wrongs and dos and don'ts make their mark on her. Her elders tell her she's wrong unless she agrees with their views, so over time she ceases to trust her own judgement.

So how were we supposed to understand that when they called us naughty or mischievous they wanted us to improve and be successful? How could we have known that by calling us bad they were trying to make us good? How could our young minds have appreciated that people who continually criticized us really had our best interests at heart?

All children experience feelings of inferiority because they are so reliant on others. Alfred Adler, a psychologist and contemporary of Sigmund Freud in the early years of this century, based an entire system of psychotherapy on the idea that our main aim in life is to overcome our childish feelings of inferiority. Adults were so much bigger and so much more capable than we were. Every time we compared ourselves with them, we felt inadequate.

. . . To Teenagers . . .

These feelings of inadequacy reached their peak in our adolescent years. We were pressured to conform, and expected to accept ideas whether we agreed with them or not, often without the opportunity to discuss them. In secondary school, we received the most emotionalized attention from authority figures when we wore the wrong coloured socks or sported a non-regulation hairstyle.

Punishments were meted out if we stepped out of line. We were given detentions for incomprehensible reasons and made to do meaningless things like writing words and phrases several hundred times over. Our intellectual and spiritual growth came a poor second to keeping out of trouble. Somehow our opinions didn't count.

Teenagers will eagerly follow trends, and strive to belong to their chosen peer group as an escape from their sense of incompetence and unworthiness. It's hardly surprising they should feel anxious about themselves, considering the pressures they are under. Most adults would have difficulty trying to cope with the combination of enormous physical changes, studying for examinations, and having to make important decisions about the future.

The Need to Perform

Have you ever noticed the way in which parents like to boast about how advanced their children are? We hear how one was walking at ten months, and how another could talk before she was eighteen months old. Parents who have low self-esteem are tempted to bask in the glow of their children's achievements.

At school, pupils who do well are admired and praised, while pressure is put on the slow learner. The hesitant reader who stumbles over a few words in class soon becomes aware of the sniggers of the other kids. Children who get poor marks, even if they are very bright but a little careless, soon get the impression that they don't count quite as much as those at the top of the class.

Some parents put enormous pressure on their children to succeed, so it's not surprising that they link their feelings of self-worth to how they perform. This belief that a person's value is in some way linked to his achievements is often carried through into adulthood.

Dave recently attended a junior school sports day. A seven-year-old girl came last in every race she entered; she fell over in the sack race, tripped over the skipping rope and couldn't quite keep the egg on the spoon. The watching crowd of parents loved her; she had a broad grin on her face throughout and was obviously enjoying herself. Meanwhile, her mother easily won the Mum's race and her Dad powered his way to a convincing victory in the Dad's event. They were later heard accusing their daughter of letting the family down.

That little girl, who had given so much pleasure to the onlookers, deserved to be congratulated for taking part so cheerfully, yet she is likely to feel for the rest of her life that her parents thought she just wasn't good enough because other children could run faster.

The eldest child in a family is often saddled with the greatest expectations, so nothing is said when he excels; after all, that's only to be expected. The youngest child, however, has problems of her own. She has to compete with older children for attention. Her elder brothers and sisters are more capable of taking care of themselves and are allowed more freedom and responsibility. Some youngest children wonder if their parents will ever let them grow up.

Even Well-Loved Children Can Develop a Poor Self-Image

The idea that children should be criticized constantly if they are to be 'well brought-up' is so ingrained that most parents do it without questioning. Some, however, realize the problems it causes, and try hard to help their children cope with the pitfalls of growing up. It seems unfair, but even children showered with love and affection can develop a poor self-image.

From the day Natalie was born, she lacked nothing materially. Every opportunity was open to her. Her wealthy parents took her on foreign holidays, sent her to the best private school and bought her a brand-new sports car on her seventeenth birthday. Her school record was impeccable: excellent reports, good at sport and a regular performer in the orchestra. She won a place at university with ease.

However, once she left the parental home, Natalie became depressed and sought help from the student counsellor. She told him that she felt totally inadequate. Much of the blame was placed at her parents' door. 'They think I'm wonderful because I've always done what they want,' she said, 'but I'm not. It's just that they don't really know me.'

Many months of counselling were devoted to Natalie's struggle with her feelings of guilt. She believed she had fooled her parents into accepting her. This is common among children whose parents have never given them love and acceptance for who they *are*, and who have not taken the trouble to try and see their point of view.

Suggestions Have Power

Suggestions made by one person to another, especially those made by someone in a position of authority, can have enormous power. Doctors who hand out placebos know that the very idea that the patient has a tablet that will 'make him better' does the trick, even if it contains no active ingredients. Similarly a parent's suggestions to a child are enough to shape that child's self-image. It doesn't even have to be spoken – the implication is quite sufficient.

We know from our own experience how damaging negative suggestions can be. 'I realized many years later that my father loved me,' says Dave, 'but I didn't think so when I was a teenager. He had worked his way up from poor beginnings to a very responsible job, and he wanted me to be even more successful. He believed that you would make a boy "soft" if you showed him any affection so he criticized everything I did, thinking he would make me try harder.

'By the time I was fourteen, I was convinced that I was no good at any of the things that mattered. One year, I did well in every school subject except one, and guess which he focused his comments on? Another school report remarked that I had become very reserved, and needless to say it provoked another battery of criticism. Funnily enough, he would tell his friends of my achievements with great pride. But he never told me.'

'I never had any praise from my parents,' says Rex, 'none at all. I was so dispirited that I used to get picked on at school. It got to the point where I was so fed up with being bullied that I left school prematurely, started work and took up karate. Only then did my self-esteem start to improve.'

Can Parents Win?

Parenting is a thankless task. If a child is given too little attention, he feels he isn't very important because Mum and Dad prefer to do something else with their time than spend it with him. On the other hand, too much attention and he feels stifled, wishing he could have more space to himself. Being a parent is the most important job we ever take on, and one of the few where there's no proper training. Most parents are caring and conscientious and do the best they can, often under very difficult conditions.

We have sons and daughters of our own and we know how hard it is. It's a fact that the times when we really give our kids the most concentrated attention is when they've done something wrong. If they are playing happily, reading or watching television, we can get on with the things we want to do and safely leave them alone. If they are amusing themselves quietly, what do we say to them? Precisely nothing! Yet if we hear them quarrelling loudly, or the sound of something breaking, we dash in to see what's happening and try to restore the peace.

So how can we possibly criticize our parents when we are behaving just like they did? They, too, had their own burdens to carry, resulting from their childhood experiences. They too were fed on a diet of criticism and starved of praise when small. Unless they consciously worked on themselves, it seems inevitable that they would treat their children the same.

It seems that even the best intentioned get it wrong, but it's no use feeling bitter about the way you were treated. It would be unfair to blame your parents because they believed they were doing their best. It is just unfortunate that few parents regard praise as the primary way of raising their children.

> *Once in a century someone may be ruined or made insufferable by praise. But surely once a minute something generous dies for want of it.*
>
> John Masefield

Motivating Children

Common sense suggests that the best way to get somebody to improve is to reward him when he does well, and point out mistakes in a constructive and helpful way. Positive feedback and selective praise are far more effective than punishment and criticism. Many parents can't help themselves pointing out all their children's weaknesses, but allow their achievements to go unnoticed because they underrate their significance.

One common reason for this is that often parents have an inherent dislike for 'big-headed' people. They criticize them for having too good an opinion of themselves and are eager to ensure that their children don't grow up that way. They (perhaps subconsciously) fear that their children may become conceited or complacent. They are keen for them to outdo the neighbours' kids, but don't want them to become arrogant and boastful. So, with the best of intentions, they spur them on to greater efforts with a verbal whip rather than the gentle persuasion of praise and encouragement.

The sad irony is that children who are given appreciation don't need to brag. They naturally feel good about themselves and don't need to prove anything to their friends.

Children deserve love and attention irrespective of what they do; it is enough that they exist. They don't have to win at games, get into the school team or come top of the class. They shouldn't have to be physically beautiful, super-intelligent or have well-off parents. But it is a fact of life that society places greater value on children who have these attributes than those who don't.

The Past Is Dead

You can choose to blame your parents for your low self-esteem, but that will achieve nothing apart from keeping you stuck in a victim pattern. Parents who have low self-esteem themselves are unlikely to be able to develop positive self-regard in their children. If you think your parents, or anyone else, have ruined your life by the way they treated you, realize that this is just a thought, and that thinking patterns can be changed. Otherwise you will never grow up or learn to trust your own feelings, and will always be making excuses instead of making the most of yourself. Whatever they did to you – or you think they did to you – forgive them.

We know some parents do terrible things to their children; mental, emotional and physical abuse are rife, and we're not saying parents who treat their children badly deserve to be forgiven; but *you* deserve not to have to live with that abuse any longer. You don't have to carry a burden of despair and guilt that is not of your doing around with you forever, and the only way to release yourself from the pain is forgiveness.

This is a crucial realization. Think about it. Bearing a grudge won't harm the other person, but it will play havoc with you. You owe it to yourself to drop it once and for all so you can get on with your life. Think about your childhood experiences, reflect on the effect you are allowing them to have on you, and work out a strategy for freeing yourself from them. The following exercises will help.

SUMMARY OF CHAPTER 5

1. Your self-esteem was established early in your life and reinforced as you grew up. Children learn by example and rely heavily on role models. Your parents and teachers had a major influence on your self-image when you were very young.
2. All children feel inferior. Most children are trained not to feel good about themselves, the majority unintentionally. This alone explains much of their behaviour, especially during the teenage years.
3. Children who think they can only win respect and admiration by conforming to others' expectations lose touch with their own feelings in the process.
4. Most parents do the best they can for their children, but those with low self-esteem are very unlikely to know how to teach their children how to feel good about themselves. If you are a parent, work on your self-esteem, not just for your own benefit, but for your children too.
5. Forgive your parents forever, unconditionally. Not because *they* deserve it, but because *you* do. If you carry on harbouring resentment, you are only damaging yourself. The past is dead, but you're not. Drop these destructive thoughts and get on with enjoying the rest of your life.

EXERCISES

1. The child you were has not evaporated; he or she lives on within
   you. Her feelings are still active in your unconscious mind. If you
   believe you had an unhappy, unsatisfying childhood your inner
   child is there, nagging away at you, hindering your growth and
   holding you back. This exercise will encourage you to come to
   terms with your inner child. Complete each of the following
   sentences with at least six endings:

   When my inner child feels ignored by me . . . .
   . . . .
   . . . .

   When my inner child feels criticized by me . . . .
   . . . .
   . . . .

   If my inner child were to feel accepted by me . . . .
   . . . .
   . . . .

   If I were to listen to my inner child he or she would say . . . .
   . . . .
   . . . .

   If I accept my inner child as an important and valuable part of
   me . . . .
   . . . .
   . . . .

   Now allow yourself to relax completely and reflect on your
   sentence endings. You will gain a valuable insight into the way
   your inner child is still influencing you.

2. This exercise uses a technique called 'reframing'. Its purpose is
   to change your mental attitude towards some event in the past
   which is still causing you distress. You cannot change what
   happened, but you can change what you *think* of the event and
   stop it troubling you any further.
       Firstly, make sure you have twenty minutes to spare and make
   yourself very comfortable. Relax your body completely. Focus
   your gaze on a fixed spot on the ceiling or wall and count slowly
   backwards from ten to one. With each number, take a deep

breath, hold it for a count of three, and as you exhale think the word 'relax'. Allow your eyes to close.

You will find your mind drifting off into the peaceful relaxed state we call 'Alpha', where your mental activity slows down and you can see things more clearly.

Now take your mind back to an event in your childhood that has made its mark on you. It could be a time when your parents treated you unfairly, an incident at school or a quarrel with a friend. Ask your unconscious mind to help you. Conjure up all the feelings and emotions you experienced at the time.

Now 'reframe' the event. Ask your unconscious mind to generate new ways of dealing with the situation. Run it through in your mind as you would have wanted it to be. For example, imagine your parents treating you as you deserved, and see or sense your response. Experience happy, contented feelings.

Work on the incident for five to ten minutes, then silently count from one to five and open your eyes. Repeat this exercise until you are no longer troubled by the memory.

You will find a reframing exercise on the relaxation tape which complements this book.

6. Dealing With Other People's Expectations

Our ability to get on with others is directly related to our self-esteem. The more we like ourselves and see ourselves as worthwhile and important, the more we appreciate and accept others and the more easily we can get along with them. People with high self-esteem, however, don't allow others' attitudes and behaviour to influence their beliefs about themselves. They judge themselves by their own criteria. It is dangerous and misleading to allow others to determine your self-worth for you.

You're going to have to learn to cope with other people's expectations, and handle criticism and rejection, if you're going to take charge of yourself. When you reach the point where you can cope confidently with these, you'll be secure within your own boundaries, and feel no need to prove anything to anybody.

Others' expectations are not really any of your business. You didn't create them and you don't own them. If you don't co-operate with someone else's plans for you that's their problem, not yours. You aren't even obliged to follow the dictates of your closest friends and relations. If they truly love you, they will want you to be yourself; they have no right to expect you to tailor yourself to suit them.

Of course, there is absolutely nothing wrong with enjoying company, being paid a compliment or receiving praise. Everyone gets pleasure from being highly thought of. But it becomes a serious problem if it is an overriding need and you allow yourself to be swayed from your chosen course because of what others say, think or do. It means that you consider *their* opinions more important than your own.

As Mark Twain once said, 'we can secure other people's

approval, if we do right and try hard; but our own is worth a hundred of it.'

> *They cannot take away our self-respect*
> *unless we give it to them.*
>
> Mahatma Gandhi

The Three Cornerstones of Self-Image

When you analyse it closely, your self-image is made up of three basic beliefs, or cornerstones, about yourself.

The first is your feeling of self-worth. This is a feeling about your relationship with yourself, whether you are worth taking care of and deserving of the good things in life. Some people instinctively feel good about themselves and accept themselves as they are, warts and all. Others feel the opposite – guilty, condemned to mediocrity, worrying all the time that they are not worth very much. The Universal Intelligence that created you (whatever you believe that to be) simply wouldn't have bothered if it didn't think you were worth it, so if you feel unworthy, *change* that feeling.

> *I am as my Creator made me, and*
> *since he is satisfied, so am I.*
>
> Minnie Smith

The second is a feeling of 'belongingness', and your ability to relate to others. Most of us need the company of other human beings and like to be accepted by those we love and admire. Not everyone has this need to the same extent, though. Some thrive on company and are only happy when surrounded by others. They feel empty or rejected on their own. Other people are quite content with their own company and prefer plenty of space to follow their own pursuits. Carl Jung, the distinguished Swiss psychologist, christened these two basic tendencies 'extroversion' and 'introversion'. We all lean one way or the other and neither is more admirable. If you are more of an introvert, that's fine for you.

The third cornerstone is competence, the ability to deal with the challenges and situations life throws at us. Some people feel capable of dealing with anything; others feel out of their depth, as though they are failures in life. Do you rise to a challenge, and enjoy facing new situations? Or do you feel uncomfortable coping with such problems? Feelings of competence can usually be traced back to feedback received from parents and teachers, feedback that has stayed buried in the unconscious mind and which often undermines adult lives years later.

The idea that most people are promoted one step higher than their level of competence at work is actually a misconception. Most of us rise as high as our self-esteem dictates, and then stop. People are not *promoted* to their level of incompetence; they find themselves one notch higher than their self-concept will permit, so they *behave* incompetently. They don't see themselves as managers of others, but they're not incompetent, just lacking in confidence.

If you find yourself in a position which you feel you can't handle and constantly tell yourself you're out of your depth, your unconscious mind will regard your negative self-talk as an instruction to get you out of the situation. You might find yourself 'inadvertently' making silly slip-ups, and be asked to return to your old job. Your conscious mind won't even be aware of what's happened!

You can deal with feelings of incompetence in several ways. You can behave as if you are helpless and hope that someone will take pity and help you out. You can withdraw completely and hope no one will notice you. You can try to please authority figures in the hope they will treat you leniently, or do the opposite – reveal your defiance through your dress and behaviour. But all these reactions are self-defeating: the only way forward is to change the thinking patterns that originally created these feelings.

Everybody has feelings of self-worth, belongingness and competence to some degree. A healthy self-image means having positive feelings in all these areas most of the time.

Conditions of Worth

The founder of non-directive counselling, Carl Rogers, regarded the tendency to worry too much about what other people think as the main source of psychological problems. The habit could, he argued, be traced to childhood, when we needed to please our parents to get what we wanted. A smile, a hug or a word of praise from Mum or Dad were worth more to us than anything else in the world. Our parents set the standards and provided the measuring stick for what was acceptable.

As adults, we are under tremendous pressure to adopt attitudes and behaviour patterns which are not necessarily our own. Rogers called these 'Conditions of Worth'. We believe that we will be rejected by those whose love and respect we most desire if we do not adhere to them.

The mainstay of Rogerian therapy is to shift the client towards setting his own standards of behaviour and relying on his own internal frame of reference. Rogers placed a lot of emphasis on this point; unless you achieve it, he maintained, you cannot become a fully functioning person.

In the Western world, society has adopted some curious norms for judging the worth of an individual. These are promoted through the media and taught to young children in school. They are communicated in many ways, some spoken and some implied. The pressures are so great that most children find it hard to resist, and the resulting feelings of inadequacy are carried forward into adulthood.

Appearances Count

The most obvious criterion for judging someone is by their appearance. Popularity is linked to attractiveness. The heroes and heroines in children's books are rarely unattractive, and characters in films and television programmes follow suit. The media convey the impression that there is an ideal size and way to dress. Advertisements feature models with all the physical qualities we are encouraged to admire.

For many, especially women, attractiveness remains a top priority throughout life. As little girls they are taught that it is essential to look pretty. As they mature, they learn that the shape of their bodies, their hair style and even the length of their nails are at least as important as their other qualities.

Men, too, are very aware that their appearance can influence others. Male politicians, for example, know that the voters are taken in by a charming smile and a natty suit and tie. Recently, one prominent politician delayed the departure of his flight, inconveniencing thousands of air travellers, when he insisted on having his hair trimmed while his plane was on the runway waiting to take off!

> *Some are born great, some achieve*
> *greatness, and some hire public*
> *relations officers.*
>
> Daniel J. Boorstin

It is particularly unfortunate that we condition children to regard physical appearance as such an important quality. The attractive child is given more attention from other children and adults. In the teenage years, the good-looking ones are more successful with the opposite sex. Young people judged ugly or plain are more likely to be ignored, which reinforces their poor self-image and leaves them with feelings which can influence them for life.

You should realize that people who follow fashions blindly are engaging in self-defeating behaviour. Just think about it; they rate themselves according to someone else's tastes, a fruitless and expensive exercise whose sole purpose is to put money in the pockets of the clothing manufacturers. It is also fraught with danger; attitudes can be very fickle, and it is hard to keep up with anyone who is constantly changing his mind. You cannot control how others think and behave, so why make yourself unhappy using an elastic measure for evaluating yourself?

The truth is that most of us do not conform to the physical norms put across in the media. By definition, half of us are taller than average, and half are shorter; half have bigger noses, and half have smaller ones. This does not devalue us in any way. Once we have decided not to be affected by it, the problem simply evaporates into thin air. Let your inner beauty shine through! Your character is more important than your appearance, which is temporary anyway. Attractive young people often lose their good looks when they reach their thirties and forties, whereas those who have always had to rely more on their personalities remain as appealing as ever.

And if you're exactly the same as everyone else, how are you to have your own identity? It is precisely those little differences which you might dislike so much which give you your special charm.

> *The advantage of doing one's own praising to oneself is that one can lay it on so thick and exactly in the right places.*
>
> Samuel Butler

Intelligence

Intelligent people attract far more admiration than those deemed to be stupid. Like so many attitudes, this one is acquired in childhood. The children with the best marks attract the teacher's approval, and are praised by their parents. Children who do not make a good impression may be branded as having low ability, and spend the rest of their lives falsely believing themselves to be unintelligent.

Researchers at Yale University came to the conclusion that only 20 per cent of a person's material success is due to academic ability and training. The rest is down to personal qualities such as persistence, creativity and determination.

Dave has taught many young people who thought they were not especially bright, but who made tremendous progress and gained good qualifications. All too often, intelligence is not assessed by the most important criterion: someone's ability to make the most of his opportunities and design a lifestyle which is rich in health, happiness and personal success. Like so many externally imposed conditions of worth, it can be a very unreliable measure for judging the true value of an individual.

The Need to Perform

Can you remember who came second to Linford Christie in the men's 100 metres sprint final at the 1992 Olympics? Probably not; yet this athlete (whose name was Frankie Fredericks) trained just as hard as Christie, and gave it his best shot on the day. Nobody would argue that he is a less worthy person.

As we have seen, many parents place enormous pressure on their children to perform at sport, music, examinations or whatever they regard as worthwhile activities, so it is not surprising many adults link their self-worth to their achievements. You don't have to do anything at all to be worthy. Convince yourself that you don't have to win, be good at anything or even do your best. Just being yourself is enough.

Money Talks

We are encouraged to believe that the wealthier members of society are somehow more creditable than the less well-off. Very young children learn that some of their friends have more toys, better clothes or bigger houses than others. Junior school children notice who arrives at school in the most expensive car, and who is able to go horse riding or ski-ing. Teenagers often sneer at classmates whose trainers don't have an expensive brand name, even if the product is just as good and the best their parents can manage.

Sometimes material wealth is earned by hard work, but not always. Talents are not shared equally among the population, and some children benefit from vast fortunes without any effort on their part. Often a family which appears to be well-off because of an expensive lifestyle is actually deeply in debt and worth less financially than a family which budgets and spends its money more prudently.

What matters is making the most of your abilities and resources. Self-worth is all about knowing that you are not wasting your talents, and are happy and successful at whatever you have chosen to do. Material wealth is a poor measure in all these respects.

Handling Criticism

It would be wonderful to be able to go through life without ever being criticized, but that is not the way of the world. Your employer regards it as his right to criticize you, and many companies have formal assessment procedures for this very purpose. Your spouse, children, friends and colleagues probably all criticize you at some time, either to your face or behind your back.

If you hear that someone has been criticizing you, you have two options. You can choose to ignore it; after all, it's only his opinion and it needn't concern you. Once you have built up your self-esteem, idle chatter won't bother you. If you feel the criticism is important enough, you can confront him.

Here are three ways of coping with deliberate put-downs. Firstly, you can take the wind out of his sails by agreeing with him:

'The house is a pig sty. You're so untidy.'

'Yes, you're quite right, I know the house needs tidying.'

Or, if you detect that the aggressor wants to upset you, you can admit calmly that there may be some truth in the accusation, but add a comment that shows you have made your own mind up about the situation:

'The house is a pig sty. It's always a mess. Don't you care? Doesn't it bother you that you're so scruffy?'

'Yes, I know it could be tidier but that's the way it's going to stay while I'm working on the garden. I'll tidy the house when I've finished.'

Thirdly, you can ask the critic a question. This will show you whether he is trying to be constructive or is just having a go at you:

'You probably won't want to take that faulty product back to the shop because you're too scared.'

'Why do you think I'm too scared?'

At this point, a put-down specialist will either duck the question or add another barbed comment, but once you've shown his intentions up you can easily deflect him. A critic who is genuinely concerned for your welfare will follow up with a helpful comment, or even a compliment.

'I've noticed you sometimes don't seem to know what to say. Why don't you try this approach? I know you've been very busy lately – would you like me to come with you?'

If your self-esteem is low, you may be taking unfair criticism. Examine each criticism carefully to decide whether it is valid. If it is not, tell the critic that you think he's being unfair. What exactly is his motive? It is quite likely that *he* has a poor self-image, and is deliberately trying to undermine your confidence for reasons of insecurity or jealousy. If he is trying to use you as a whipping boy, that's his problem. Don't let it become yours.

A person with a poor self-image may also react to criticism aggressively, which is self-defeating since the exchange usually ends up as a slanging match, and heated arguments rarely get anyone anywhere. Remember, when others criticize you, it's because they regard you as a worthy target. If they're not criticizing you, you haven't arrived yet!

However you choose to respond to criticism, always assert your right to be the judge of your own actions. You could politely thank the critic for her comments and say that you'll deal with the situation in your own way.

Leslie was over-weight, taking anti-depressants and tranquillizers and was unhappy with his home life. The problem boiled down to his relationship with his wife, who constantly criticized and insulted him. He had allowed her to affect his already low self-esteem. Rex introduced him to the Dynamic Living Principles.

Gradually, Leslie began to see himself differently, and realized it was worth the effort to work on himself. He joined a gym and changed his eating habits. His energy level rose dramatically. As his self-esteem started to improve, he developed the confidence to take a firm stand. He made it clear to his wife that he would not allow her to treat him that way, and they were able to resolve the situation. Now, he has far greater self-respect, has come off the anti-depressants and is enjoying life to the full.

Forgiveness

Many of us are laden with a heavy and unnecessary load, which we lug about grimly from day to day. This burden is labelled 'past resentments', and is a collection of bitter thoughts about how we've been mistreated by our parents, teachers, work-mates and so on.

We feel the need to punish them somehow, and so we keep these feelings alive, feeding them with our imaginations and fantasies of revenge. If we are suffering, why shouldn't they? In reality, of course, we are harming no one but ourselves, and even though in our rational moments we can see this quite clearly, we often find it difficult to control our resentment.

The answer is forgiveness. By forgiving them you set yourself free. After all, who are you hurting by harbouring all that emotional garbage? Certainly not *them*. Simply let it go – and stop punishing yourself today for something done to you months or even years ago.

Giving the Right Signals

If others are treating you badly, you are probably consciously or unconsciously giving out the wrong signals. You might be indicating that you don't think much of yourself, enjoy being treated like a door-mat, or won't stand up for yourself in an argument. Well, if that's how you feel, how can you expect anyone else to think differently? Stop destroying yourself! Choose to be a fully functioning person, and people will soon sense that you are a force to be reckoned with. Their respect for you will increase in line with your respect for yourself.

Assertiveness

Assertiveness is a popular word that is often misunderstood. It does *not* mean being aggressive, pushy or loud. It is simply a way of communicating our wants and feelings to others clearly and confidently, without manipulating, intimidating or hurting them in the process. In other words, it is making ourselves understood, taking a stand when necessary, while showing our respect for the other person. It does not involve being evasive, calling people names, agreeing with a point of view we do not accept or verbally battering the other person into submission.

To be assertive, you must practise expressing your feelings in a firm but relaxed manner. You must not be afraid to give or receive compliments, ask for what you want or take the occasional risk that someone will refuse you or take a different stance. You must create your own space that others will respect, while acknowledging their right to do the same.

Dynamic Living techniques (see Chapters 10 and 11) can help you to become more assertive in many ways. For instance, you can take the sting out of any forthcoming situation by rehearsing it in your mind beforehand. You can use affirmations to reinforce your awareness that you are an assertive person, reframe incidents from the past where you felt you had let yourself down, and use auto-suggestion and relaxation to recondition your unconscious mind.

SUMMARY OF CHAPTER 6

1. People with high self-esteem do not allow others' attitudes and behaviour to influence their beliefs about themselves. They know that their own expectations are what matter.
2. Avoid judging yourself by others' standards. Set your own.
3. Society generally sees appearance, intelligence and financial wealth as the main standards for judging a person's worth. Don't be fooled; these are superficial measures.
4. Learn to handle criticism. You can't expect others to treat you as you desire all the time, so train yourself to become immune to whatever they throw at you.
5. Learn to behave assertively. Stand up for yourself.

EXERCISE: ANCHORING

Make yourself comfortable, and relax your body and mind. Let your thoughts drift back to a time when you were with other people, perhaps at a social event or in a work situation, when you felt really good about yourself. See and hear yourself at ease, laughing and joking or putting your point of view across convincingly. Conjure up the emotions you were experiencing at the time.

Now put the thumb and fingers of either your left or right hand together as you hold the impression firmly in your mind.

Next time you encounter a similar situation, put the thumb and fingers together again and you will feel a surge of positive emotions which will not only help you to cope but will also create another success.

Anchoring can help you deal with any forthcoming event about which you feel uneasy, but only if you practise. Remember, 'use it, or lose it'.

7. Understanding Yourself

Everybody has the potential to raise their self-esteem, no matter how it stands at the moment. There is always some area of your life or some skill or ability that could be improved. But you need to be aware of your present beliefs, attitudes and thinking patterns before you can start to improve them.

This chapter will help you to assess your current self-image. There are six groups of questions corresponding to the five key life areas – physical and health, finance and career, relationships, recreation and leisure, spiritual growth and self-development – plus general questions exploring your attitudes to yourself and your life.

Answer each question as honestly as you can. You will find it useful to work through them again after thirty days, then again six months and one year from now so you can see the positive changes which have occurred.

Spend some time on this exercise. We know that each question could be answered by a straightforward 'yes' or 'no', but you will only get the full benefit if you write a short explanation. For example, to question 3, 'Do I eat properly?', you could simply answer 'yes' or 'no,' but a comment like 'Sometimes I lapse when I'm out with my friends,' or 'I enjoy a healthy diet except I am partial to chocolate,' would throw additional light on the matter.

It is important to write down your answers. The act of committing ideas to paper reinforces them, and stimulates your unconscious mind to find ways of taking advantage of opportunities and offering solutions to problems. It also provides an interesting record for the future.

Above all, enjoy this exercise. Questionnaires can be great fun, and you have the added incentive of knowing that you are working to improve your self-esteem and changing your life circumstances.

Physical and Health

1. Is health a top priority for me?
2. Am I satisfied with my current state of health and my physical appearance?
3. Do I eat properly?
4. Do I take regular exercise?

Finance and Career

5. Am I able to earn my living doing what I enjoy?
6. If not, do I have a plan for changing the work I do to something I would find more rewarding?
7. Do I have all the money I need to do what I want with my life?
8. Do I like taking responsibility?
9. Do I begrudge others their success?

Relationships

10. Have I unconditionally forgiven my parents for any anguish they caused me when I was younger?
11. Am I satisfied with my intimate relationships with others, including my marriage and/or my love life?
12. Do I look at people when I talk to them?
13. Can I share my attitudes and ideas with others without embarrassment, and stick to my opinions irrespective of what other may say or do?
14. Do I know how to give and receive love?
15. Do I have a good circle of friends?
16. Do I know how to win new friends and keep the friends I value?
17. Do I avoid criticizing others, even to myself?
18. Do I feel comfortable dealing with others who criticize me?

Recreation and Leisure

19. Do I have fun and enjoy myself often enough?
20. Have I struck a good balance between work and leisure, so that I am able to relax and recharge my batteries?
21. Do I have a hobby, or hobbies, which provide me with the enjoyment and creative expression I need?
22. Do I take regular holidays?

Spiritual Growth and Self-Development

23. Do I have a sense of purpose in my life which benefits others as well as myself?
24. Do I have a plan for building into myself the qualities I need to be successful?
25. Do I tune in to and feel at one with the Power within me?

General

26. Do I like myself?
27. Do I avoid criticizing myself?
28. Am I confident about my intellectual abilities?
29. When I look in the mirror, do I respect the person I see?
30. Is the person I see someone who I really want to be?

If you can answer 'yes' with reasonable certainty to all thirty questions, give this book to a friend – you obviously don't need it! More than twenty-four and your self-esteem is high. Fifteen or more suggests that you have reasonable self-esteem, but with a little effort and persistence you could raise it significantly. Under fifteen and you have work to do!

We suggest you buy a small notebook. Label it your 'self-esteem' diary. Fill in your responses to these questions (and any others which may come to mind). Read through it every day, reflect on its contents and keep it up-to-date with any thoughts you have as you make progress.

If you have answered these questions honestly, you already

have a good idea of what you are like. But beware; completing a questionnaire is a *conscious* activity which makes use of the left side of your brain: the rational, logical side. If you aren't aware of the structure of the mind, you will discover in Chapter 8 that each of us operates on two mental levels, the conscious and the unconscious, and has two hemispheres within the brain which we call the right and left-hand sides. If you are lacking in confidence, you probably have some destructive, negative material stored in your unconscious mind which needs to be revealed so you can stop it from influencing you.

As well as the exercises in Chapter 10, the cassette tapes which complement this book will help you to access your unconscious and recondition it for a positive self-image and bags of self-confidence. Read on and you will discover how to use your mind to develop an understanding of the real you – not your self-concept, or self-image, but the *real* person who is waiting to appear and change the direction of your life for the better!

8. It's All In The Mind

Psychologists have cited low self-esteem as the prime cause of a wide range of neurotic conditions: fear of intimacy or success; alcohol, tobacco and drug abuse; underachievement at school or at work; child abuse; spouse battering; sexual dysfunctions; emotional immaturity; suicidal tendencies; crimes of violence, and many more. We know that all these problems, and more, can be tackled once you have a working knowledge of the mechanics of the mind.

This chapter describes the workings of the mind and explains how you can bring about any changes you desire. Re-read it until you have grasped its implications. Your self-esteem is made up of nothing more than a collection of powerful thoughts, which shape your life for good or ill. With practice, however, you can choose your thoughts and change negative to positive at will.

Breaking the Spiral

If you are going to improve your self-esteem, you must consciously break the Spiral of Despair. It doesn't really matter where you start; every positive change you make will influence the next step, which in turn will affect the step after that, and so on, until the Spiral comes round again. The important thing is to begin. You could decide to start by doing something that interests you well, and then savour your own success. You are bound to receive positive feedback from others, which will improve your self-image, so you do even better next time, and so on.

If you create a feeling of confidence in yourself, others will be aware of it and will instinctively treat you with more respect,

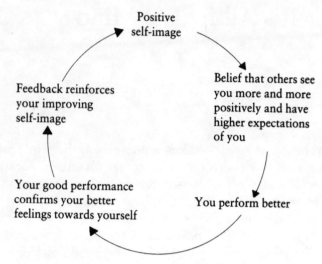

Figure 2.   *Reversing the Circle of Despair*

and so you will become more confident. So from now on behave *as if* you have a good self-image. Others will then see you more positively, which in turn will motivate you to accomplish something worthwhile.

Thoughts Are Things

Thoughts have tremendous power; every action you have ever taken began as a thought. You cannot breathe, talk, eat, move or blink without a conscious or unconscious thought entering your mind, even if only for a fraction of a millisecond. Every one of your emotions – happiness, sadness, anger, guilt, shame originates as a thought.

During a typical day, thousands of thoughts go through your head. Most float in and out quite innocuously, but those which take hold can either be very harmful, or can do you a great deal of good. It all depends on which ones you allow to flourish in your mind.

*You cannot stop birds flying overhead. But
you can stop them from nesting in your hair.*

Anon

We all need to understand the power of thought. Your thoughts can build you up, or destroy you. They have an enormous effect on your body and your life. But sadly, most of us find it very hard to hold a positive thought for more than a few seconds, yet a negative thought can stay with us for days on end. No wonder most people are not as happy as they could be!

Scientists estimate that 80 per cent of your energy is used up by the thoughts floating round in your head. How do they get there in the first place? The answer is simple: you put them there. You, perhaps unknowingly, choose which thoughts to hold on to and which to banish.

Your self-esteem is only a collection of thoughts about yourself, based to a large extent on your past experience. The good news is that you *can* control and change your thoughts. If you don't do this, they will control you. Learn to channel them correctly and you will have the power to improve your self-image and reshape your life.

The Law of Cause and Effect

Every cause has an effect. The 'cause' in your life is always a thought, and the result, or 'effect', is usually an action. Every action, in turn, has an effect on your life, however small. A kind of chain reaction is set up.

If you have right causes you will get right results. Wrong causes will lead to wrong results. It's as simple as that. Your long-term destiny is really only a result of your behaviour minute by minute, day by day, and your behaviour is always a result of the thoughts which preceded it. If you allow yourself to be influenced by indiscriminate negative input, you're creating a poor self-image and a lack of self-confidence, because your mind is still untrained and has no firm direction.

Ask yourself: What do I want to achieve? What is my ultimate destiny? Since your present goal is to raise your self-esteem, ask yourself: What will I have to think, believe and do every minute of every day, to improve my self-image and confidence?

Being aware of the power of thought, and the inevitability of cause and effect, will set you on the road to success. If you want the right results, you must think the right thoughts.

The Left and Right Hemispheres of the Brain

We can regard the brain as having two parts, or hemispheres, each having its own special functions.

The Left Brain, or Conditioned Mind, deals with analysing, logic and evaluating. It processes words and numbers, controls your use of language and your ability to think in a structured, rational way. It is rather limited since it can only process one piece of information at a time.

In contrast, the Right Brain, or Reflective Mind, is the intuitive, creative side. It operates in pictures, and it senses rather than thinks. It doesn't rely on material from the past, and it can handle an unlimited amount of information at any one time, so it doesn't have the restrictions of the Left Brain. It knows what is right and what is wrong; it can see the link between cause and effect without judging, criticizing or condemning.

Although most people have a tendency to favour one side or the other, we all alternate between the two modes depending on what we are doing. If we are reading, speaking or doing calculations, our Left Brain is engaged and the Right Brain temporarily quietened. If we are painting, listening to music, creating new ideas or using our 'sixth sense', we are relying on our Right Brain and inhibiting the Left.

Alpha Level

All of our behaviour is based on old habit patterns, almost as if a videotape recorder in your mind is constantly recording everything that happens to you – not just what you see and hear, but all your feelings and emotions too. These recordings will influence your actions and your thoughts if you let them.

The Left Brain will continually race from one thought to the next, wreaking havoc with our self-image since it is conditioned by all our bad memories from the past. Fortunately, you can use your Right Brain to reprogramme your Conditioned Left Brain. This is done by quietening your Left Brain and allowing the Right Brain, which is normally pushed into the background by the Left during your daytime activities, to exert its influence.

Luckily there is a simple method of achieving this. It involves getting into the relaxed state known as 'Alpha Level', which is the dreamy, semi-conscious phase we all pass through last thing at night and first thing in the morning. It is a state of total relaxation and heightened mental awareness.

Once in Alpha, the mind is quiet, but also very powerful because the reflective Right Brain can observe the chattering and chasing Left Brain, reflect on what it sees, and start to bring about the necessary changes.

Ideally, we should use our Right Brain to produce the germ of an idea and our Left Brain to bring it to fruition. Thomas Edison, the great inventor, would sit in a quiet place until he was totally relaxed. He would allow his mind to slow down and tune into the full power of his Right Brain. He would then take the ideas that popped into his head and put them into practice.

Chapter 10 gives you many ways of relaxing and getting to Alpha Level. This is a vital skill which improves with practice. Investing a few minutes morning and evening in developing this ability would without doubt be your best investment ever!

The Conscious and Unconscious Minds

The mind can be compared to an iceberg floating in the sea. The conscious mind is the 10 per cent which is visible above the surface, housing the thinking process which you are normally aware of; the unconscious mind is the 90 per cent below, hidden but always capable of making an impact.

The conscious mind, like the Left Brain, can only process one item of information at a time. For example, if someone tried to talk to you while you were reading this book you would have to stop reading or you wouldn't hear what he said. Your conscious mind cannot pay attention to both at the same time.

The unconscious operates on two levels. Just below the surface of consciousness is the *sub*conscious mind. It consists of material which can be brought to consciousness when we want it, such as telephone numbers, names, places and dates which we can recall when we need to.

The *un*conscious is the most powerful part of the mind, even though it is completely submerged. It drives you all the time, even when you're asleep. It regulates your body (controlling your heartbeat and breathing, and so on) without you thinking about it consciously, and acts as a store of all your memories.

The unconscious is conditioned by its experiences from the moment we are born and, some would say, before we were born. Carl Gustav Jung believed that we not only have our own personal store of information in the Personal Unconscious, but also have access to all the lessons learned by our ancestors, on a deeper level of the mind he called the Collective Unconscious.

Our self-esteem, confidence, fears and all the other material that make up our psyche are programmed into the unconscious mind, and reveal themselves as a collection of habit patterns. We function according to our past conditioning, and in that respect we are victims of our perception of the past.

Sometimes the memories in the unconscious are so painful that the mind deliberately represses them. If they stay there, hidden, they influence your behaviour without your even being aware of them. The only way to release yourself from their effects is to bring them back into consciousness and work through them.

Edgar Cayce, undoubtedly the greatest psychic of this century, once said, 'The mind is the builder and the mind is the destroyer.' King Solomon is quoted in the Bible as saying, 'As a man thinketh in his heart, so is he.' Both were referring to the unconscious mind.

There is some overlap between the conscious mind and the Left Brain, and the unconscious mind and the Right Brain, but this is not important here. You don't need to know how an engine works in order to drive a car. Similarly, if you grasp the basic principles and incorporate them into your life, you will be able to use them for your benefit.

Using Your Unconscious Positively

When you use the Dynamic Living Formula, and drift down into Alpha Level and use visualization and affirmations to re-condition the unconscious mind, you are actually re-recording the 'videotapes of the mind'. You are wiping out the old destructive, negative thought patterns and building new, positive ones about yourself into the psyche.

Once you grasp this concept, you will have an exciting and powerful tool at your disposal. Changing your unconscious conditioning means you are changing yourself, and can transform your life.

The Conditioned Mind

The Left Brain relies on past experiences for its information, and is conditioned by the pleasure or pain it associated with them. Since you cannot rely on the past to solve today's problems, the Conditioned Mind makes mistakes and can be a liability. We have all been in situations where we chose to rely on memories of past events rather than following our intuition, and wished we hadn't.

Your intuition is really a direct message from your Right Brain, and is an infallible guide. Sometimes it takes courage to follow it, when 'logical' thought is insisting that you should move in another direction; but this is just the conditioned Left Brain at work.

When this happens it is important to find a quiet moment, go into Alpha Level and listen to what the reflective Right Brain is telling you. It will calm the Left Brain, correct the damaging input, and feed clear, positive thoughts into your unconscious.

The Reflective Mind

The Reflective Mind, unlike the Conditioned Mind, does not rely on material from the past. It can see the link between cause and effect with crystal clarity; it can even see the results of actions and thoughts before they occur. It observes what is happening without judging, criticizing or condemning.

People who have developed the power of their Reflective Minds have an instinct for what is right for them, and often seem to be able to see into the future. If they are aware of a destructive, self-deprecating thought entering their heads, they know how to eradicate it immediately. They seem to know exactly what to do without having to analyse all the pros and cons.

You are about to discover and release the power of your Reflective Mind! Go frequently into Alpha Level and activate your Right Brain. It then observes and mirrors the conditioning of your Left Brain, and sets the process of un-conditioning and re-conditioning in motion. Clear out the old habit patterns and replace them with the thoughts *you* choose.

Unconscious Attitudes Determine Your Circumstances

The thoughts you choose filter into your unconscious mind where they control you. Grasp the enormity of this truth and you will realize that it is without doubt the most exciting idea you have ever come across. Just imagine the potential! The great men and women of history all knew how to use this power. This insight, backed up by determination and perseverance, is the fundamental difference between greatness and mediocrity.

You can change your world by selecting positive thoughts and feeding them into your unconscious; your unconscious will then work to make those positive thoughts a reality.

Believe it or not, you've actually been unconsciously creating your present circumstances all your life without realizing it. If most of your conditioning was negative, the chances are you have created mainly negative circumstances. If you can control your thoughts, you can consciously create the circumstances you want in your life.

Your Unconscious Mind Cannot Distinguish Between Thoughts and Events

Your mind cannot tell the difference between impressions detected by your five senses (hearing, sight, smell, taste and touch), and the thoughts you allow into it. If you imagine vividly enough that you are running a marathon, your unconscious mind will accept it as a fact.

This is an important principle because it means that we can 'recondition' our minds by choosing to have different thoughts, and explains why techniques such as reframing and visualization are so effective. If you are unhappy about a past event you can, when in Alpha Level, put a different interpretation on it. Simply instruct your mind to recreate the memory of the episode and 'see' the event going the way you would have wanted it to.

We are not saying that you can change the event itself, but you can change your beliefs about it so it is no longer a burden. When Dave was fifteen years old, he was brutally attacked by a group of skinheads. While six of them pushed him to the ground and kicked him, many more stood around to make sure he didn't retaliate. His injuries took weeks to heal, and he still has some of the scars.

Although the physical bruising had long cleared, the mental bruising remained, and for a time he was wary of going where there were groups of young people. He consciously decided to view the whole incident as a learning experience. He realized that the skinheads were actually cowards who would have such incidents on their conscience for the rest of their lives. They hadn't really harmed him, but themselves. Now he feels no need to avoid groups of young people. The memories of the original event don't bother him anymore.

One useful exercise is to go through the events of the day every evening, when in Alpha Level, and see everything working out to your satisfaction. If something didn't go the way you would have liked, feed whatever would make you feel better about it into your mind. Your unconscious will accept them without judgement or criticism, because, in Alpha, the 'critical censor' which normally operates while you are awake shuts down, allowing your new thoughts to take hold.

Go into Alpha Level on a regular basis and feed in more and more positive and helpful thoughts. Recondition your mind on a step-by-step basis. **You will wonder how you ever managed before!**

> *If you think you can, or you think you can't, you're quite right.*
>
> Henry Ford

The Thinker Thinks and the Prover Proves

The mind has a way of convincing itself that it is right. If an idea seems reasonable and the mind accepts it as true, it tends to become reality. If you believe you're going to make something happen, then it will come to pass, providing you really do believe it. If you think you can't do something, you *expect* to fail and you inevitably will. It is almost as if there are two voices in your head chattering away to each other. The Thinker thinks, 'I'm no good at this, I can't do it.' The Prover sets to work making it come true. 'You see, I was right, I couldn't do it.'

Take, for example, a sports team which has lost its confidence. A cricket team can be in the final of the World Cup, then lose a few matches and receive a lot of negative criticism from the press, spectators and friends. Things snowball until, six months later, it loses ten test matches in a row and is branded a national disgrace. The players go onto the field believing they're going to lose, and somehow manage to snatch defeat from the jaws of victory one way or another.

If you allow the Thinker to think 'I'm a useless, stupid person,' the Prover will seek the proof and it won't be disappointed. On the other hand, if you think you can and believe it, then you will set about proving that you can.

When Avril was a fifteen-year-old she had to change schools six months before sitting her GCSE exams. Her family moved to another part of the country where they discovered the schools were using a different syllabus, and the subjects were not synchronized. The local school refused to take her, as the head teacher insisted there was no chance of Avril passing her exams at the end of the year because she had not done the work already covered by the school. 'Even if a girl was outstanding, it could not be done,' said the head, grimly examining Avril's uninspiring grades from her previous school, 'And I'm afraid I cannot risk lowering my school's reputation by increasing the failure rate.'

Avril was indignant and angry, but she decided not to accept the head's opinion of her inability to pass. When a school was finally found, she worked hard. Contrary to everyone's expectations except her own, six months later she achieved high grades in every subject. Because she believed wholeheartedly that she *could* do it, and had enough self-esteem not to be deterred by someone else's opinion, her entire psyche was geared towards success. With that attitude, Avril couldn't fail!

The Prover has no initiative of its own, so if you make sure the Thinker is feeding it positive thoughts, the Prover will automatically make sure they materialize and you'll always win through in the long term. If you constantly *think* you can, then you must and will succeed; and the more you succeed, the more you will build your self-confidence.

Take Charge of Your Thoughts

If you want high self-esteem, consciously think good thoughts about yourself and believe them wholeheartedly. Write down all your positive attributes and read the list every day. For extra impact, recite them onto a cassette tape and play it constantly.

If you want more self-confidence, choose thoughts such as 'I will,' and 'I know I can,' and immerse yourself in them. Eliminate 'can't' or 'won't' from your vocabulary. Keep your mind focused on the positive and you will become the successful, confident person you want to be. In this way, you can consciously undo all those years of conditioning, see life the way you want to see it and discard those redundant ideas of how life *has* to be.

Never forget that if you really want to achieve excellence you will have to work very hard, just like Stephen Hendry. Learning any new skill takes practice, but once it becomes a habit you won't have to think about it consciously any more.

Stephen Hendry was the youngest World Snooker Champion ever. For as long as he can remember, he wanted to be World Champion. He set his heart on this goal and worked steadily towards it. He practised for five hours a day and became totally absorbed in snooker so that his thoughts, words and actions were all geared towards winning the championship.

He has since been World Champion four times and has earned over £3 million. But the money is just a bonus. Being World Champion and earning his living doing what he enjoys most is far more important to him.

And he *still* practises for six hours a day!

Do you remember when you first learned to ride a bicycle?

Originally you were **unconsciously incompetent**; you didn't know you couldn't do it, and it probably didn't matter to you. Once you decided to learn and sat on the saddle for the first time, you were all too aware of your inability. You wondered how you were ever going to balance, turn the pedals and steer all at the same time. You had become **consciously incompetent**.

As you progressed, you realized you could become good if you practised. You went out riding as often as possible. Sometimes it required lots of concentration, but it was worth it for the thrill of getting it right for the first few times. At that stage you were **consciously competent**. Then as you practised it became so natural you didn't even have to think; you had become **unconsciously competent**.

If you want to change all that programming and record over those old tapes you will have to try hard and be constantly on your guard against setbacks at first. But don't berate yourself. After a while it becomes easier, and eventually you find you are unconsciously and automatically being positive. But the really exciting part comes when you realize that your circumstances are definitely beginning to improve!

SUMMARY OF CHAPTER 8

1. Your self-esteem is just a collection of thoughts about yourself. Since you can control your thoughts, you can choose your own feelings of self-worth.

2. Every 'cause' has an 'effect'. Thoughts are causes, actions are effects. Right thinking inevitably leads to right actions.

3. The brain has two hemispheres: the logical, rational Left, and the intuitive, creative Right. Your mind has a conscious element and an unconscious.

4. You can learn to quieten the conscious mind and the Left Brain by going into 'Alpha Level'. This allows your intuitive and creative abilities to surface. Most of the great characters of history understood this capacity and used it to the full.

5. Your unconscious mind does not know the difference between thoughts, imagination, and external events, so you can change

your perceptions of those events by feeding in the right thoughts and impressions.

6. The Thinker thinks and the Prover proves. Take charge of the Thinker. The thoughts you choose filter into your unconscious mind where they control your destiny.

EXERCISE

This exercise should be performed as often as you can during your waking hours. At frequent intervals, listen carefully to the incessant chattering of your conscious mind. How much of your self-talk is positive? How much is negative?

Whenever you become aware of unconfident, fearful thoughts, say to yourself, inwardly or out loud, 'Stop! Cancel!' Send the harmful thought away and replace it with a confident, helpful one. For example, replace 'I can't' with 'I can', or 'She's better than me' with 'I'm just as good as her.'

This exercise takes continual practice, but after a while it becomes automatic, and after two or three weeks you will start to notice a difference. The effort is well worth it – you are actually reshaping your future!

9. You Are All You Need

Some people think it's wrong to love yourself, but we disagree. Self-love is quite different from narcissism, which is being in love *with* yourself. Loving yourself is a very important step to developing high self-esteem. Once you have it, you can share it and make others feel good about themselves too. And you'll find you are too busy getting on with your own life to worry about what others think of you.

Work On Your Most Important Relationship

We all seek fulfilling relationships with others, but have you ever stopped to think which relationship is the most important? The most crucial relationship you will ever have is the one with yourself. The secret of happiness is to cultivate and enjoy a lifelong friendship with the inner you. You may enjoy close friendships with others, but none is as longstanding or as close as your intimacy with yourself.

This was the first relationship you ever formed, and probably the only one you will share for the rest of your life. You are with yourself every minute of every day, so strive to be your own best friend and show yourself all the kindness and consideration that you would expect from others. Enjoy your own company. Find lots of reasons to be proud to be you.

This is only possible if you believe you're worth it. Your self-worth is not conditional on your achievements, and you don't have to be right all the time or never make mistakes. If you have difficulty accepting this idea, keep reading! Any misconception can and should be changed, especially one as damaging as this.

You Can't Love Yourself Too Much

There is a tendency in a nation which prides itself on its tolerance and modesty, to view people who love themselves as egotistical, selfish and rather unpleasant. We are steeped in a religious tradition which highlights sin, guilt and unworthiness and encourages self-effacement. 'How can I love myself?', we think, 'I know too much about me.'

Self-love should not be confused with false pride or conceit. Big egos do not mean high self-esteem; it's quite the opposite. Vanity and arrogance are usually just a form of bravado. It may seem a contradiction, but egotistical people actually love themselves too little. Why else would they talk as they do, unless they have something to cover up?

The loudmouth who boasts about his achievements, or what he is going to achieve, and the big talker who is always full of ideas but never puts any of them into practice, are both lacking in self-confidence and inner approval at a deeper level. Their outward behaviour is just a cover. A successful, well-balanced person has no need to boast.

The need to be loved is basic to human survival. If you aren't loved you will die, just as surely as if you were starved of food or denied shelter. It doesn't matter if this love comes from yourself or other people, as long as your 'love needs' have been taken care of. Just imagine that delicious sense of freedom! You want others to love you unconditionally, but if they don't you can manage perfectly well on your own. Unconditional love means not wanting to change the object of your love in any way; it means accepting yourself exactly as you are.

Loving someone, including yourself, is, after all, a decision you take. You don't 'fall in love'. Nobody pushes you into it; you learn to love as you grow up, and decide who to offer your love to. Like every decision, emotion and action it begins as a thought which takes root in your mind!

Please don't think we are preaching a selfish philosophy. You can't give away what you do not have, whether money, time or love. You can't give love unless you have some to give. It is impossible to love someone else if you don't think of yourself as a worthy person. There is no such thing as a person who loves him or herself too much. Love and accept yourself!

You Are Lovable As You Are

Another fallacy which causes a lot of unhappiness is the idea that you need to change yourself in order to be loved: 'If only I were slimmer, more intelligent, more beautiful, taller/shorter, wittier . . .', or 'Tomorrow, once I've learned to cook, mend cars, play tennis . . . *then* I'll be lovable, *then* I'll be happy.' So what happens when tomorrow never comes?

People who feel like this are likely to feel intimidated by others who appear to have the qualities they would like. If you feel you are too poor to be loved, you will feel inferior to those who have money; if you feel too plain to be loved, you will feel uncomfortable with those whom you see as more beautiful. You may constantly feel a desperate need to follow the latest fashions, or rush out and buy the latest trendy gadgets advertised on TV. You may be willing to lay your true opinions to one side in an effort to belong to the group.

Real love is not conditional. You don't have to prove anything, climb Everest, run a four minute mile, make a number one hit record or become a millionaire to be worth loving. You're alright because you're alright; you're alright because you're *you*.

You Don't Have To Do Your Best

Nor do you have to be perfect. The most loved person in the world makes mistakes; it's probably how he learned to be lovable in the first place.

Perfectionism, as Churchill so wisely pointed out, can make you procrastinate. You're so afraid of not reaching your own impossibly high standards you'd rather not try at all. It can make you hesitate before trying new things, so you miss out on many of life's more enjoyable experiences. It can make you shy and withdrawn because you can't risk saying something which might not be quite right.

The one thing that the most successful people in history have in common is that they all knew failure. The great inventor Thomas Edison tried and failed to invent an electric light bulb over ten thousand times, but didn't regard himself as a failure. He just carried on, knowing that every attempt took him nearer to his final goal.

Your self-worth is totally independent of your achievements. Continually using your performance as a measure of your self-esteem means you have missed the point; you do not have to win, or do your best, or do anything at all to be a worthy person. There is only one failure, and that is giving up altogether.

Don't Dwell On Your Faults

If the average person is asked to list all her strengths and weaknesses, she will effortlessly jot down dozens of bad points and struggle to find a mere handful of good ones. Even successful business people have little trouble producing long lists of their own faults, but can only generate a few positive attributes.

Why is this so? We put it down to two main reasons; our programming as children, and our willingness to allow other people's opinions to influence us too much. We constantly brood over all this negative input until we believe it is true. Reconditioning our minds by choosing positive and uplifting thoughts about ourselves takes know-how, practice and commitment.

If you dwell on your faults, you set up a chain reaction in your mind which leads to them being reinforced. Constantly saying to yourself, 'I am weak, I am a coward, stupid,' and so on will only attract more of the same. Think of strength, courage, and intelligence. Keep these qualities in your mind, and make them a part of your thinking. Remember, a fault is only a fault if you have decided that it is so.

We're not saying you must stay exactly as you are, unless your life is already a model of health, happiness and success (in which case you're one in a million). Loving yourself is not a recipe for inertia; it's quite the opposite. When you love yourself you will take the time to improve on the things you need to do better, because you know it's worth making the effort on someone as wonderful as you. Moreover, you will decide what to do for yourself, and refuse to be pushed around.

> *A man who doubts himself is like a*
> *man who enlists in the ranks of the*
> *enemy and bears arms against himself.*
> *He makes his failures certain by being*
> *the first to be convinced of it.*
>
> Alexandre Dumas

Stewart was a bright young man who had a poor self-image. He sat the entrance examination for a grammar school place and was given a mark of 96. The mark wasn't explained in the letter, so he thought it must be an IQ score. He knew 100 was the average in these tests, so assumed he was below average. As a result, his performance at the new school caused his teachers some concern, and he was asked to see the year tutor. He discovered from the tutor that the mark actually meant that he had done better than 96 per cent of all the candidates, so he was among the most able students in the school.

Needless to say, once he realized his mistake his performance improved dramatically. As we said in the last chapter, every cause has an effect. Stewart had interpreted the mark as evidence of his inadequacy because of his low self-esteem. His Prover had sought the evidence which would confirm his negative feelings about himself, but once that misconception was removed, his mind switched to proving that he was, indeed, very capable.

Identifying faults is not always a bad thing, however, since it helps you realize that you need to eliminate them and reduce their power. But beware! Unless you are really motivated to change them, you will interpret everything that happens to you as proof that you are riddled with weaknesses.

Make it a rule never to say or think anything about yourself that you don't sincerely *desire* to be true.

Sticks and Stones . . .

When you were a child you were more sensitive than you are now. If someone called you names, your immediate reaction was to retaliate with an even ruder one. This could go on for a whole playtime! Your thoughts probably went something like this: 'That boy has just been rude to me and I don't like it, so if I call him an even ruder name I'll feel as if I've got my own back on him.' You found, though, that you hadn't really resolved the situation.

If you told your mother when you got home, she would tell you that 'Sticks and stones may break my bones, but words can never hurt me.' It might have made you feel better for a while, but unfortunately it wasn't true then, and isn't true now. The effects of name-calling can be traumatic.

If you have a poor self-image, another person can easily hurt you. He only has to call you a rude name to bring about no less than a hundred physical changes in your body in under one second! If you perceive his tone of voice and gestures as threatening, you arouse yourself for a 'flight or fight' response. Your heart starts to pound, your pulse races and you get an uncomfortable feeling in your stomach. You may be so frightened that you are rendered speechless.

If this is your usual response to any sign of disapproval or aggression it can lead to serious physical and psychological problems, because tension is generated and stored within the body. It can result in, for example, headaches, neuralgia, allergies, insomnia, digestive disorders and even cancer.

You should realize that other people, however unpleasant, only have the power to upset you if you give in. If you respond with the thought, 'I'm going to react to this situation by being angry or upset,' you have handed them control.

Imagine what would happen if you had a real enemy who hated the sight of you, and was determined to make your life as miserable as possible. He wouldn't need to physically assault you; he'd just have to call you a rude name in a spiteful way, and you would crumble. You would have relinquished control of your body and mind, and handed it over to another.

Usually, if someone attacks you, it's because he's hurting inside. Young people who are caught vandalizing other people's property, or joyriding in stolen cars, often turn out to be from deprived backgrounds. Sadly, these youngsters have never enjoyed the security of a loving home, and have not yet learned to deal with the pain they feel inside. There is little that can be done unless they realize where they are going wrong, and decide to change. Then and only then, can they be helped.

It is unrealistic to expect everyone to treat you as you would like. Other people will act as they see fit for their own reasons, and you're setting yourself up for a big disappointment if you think you can change them. They are not to be pitied, condemned or patronized; they just *are*.

Above all, don't allow hurt or anger to ferment in your mind. These thoughts will not alter anyone else's thinking. Others will carry on doing as they wish regardless of what you do, say or think. Your negative thinking can only harm you.

Blowing in the Wind

It is a fact of life that many people will only offer their approval to people who share their beliefs, and withold it from anyone who does not. Unless you are confident, you will always be tempted to duck and weave as others try to talk you round to their point of view.

We know many people like this; Paul, for example, a teacher in his mid-forties, gladly expresses an opinion on any subject whenever the opportunity arises, but always makes sure his ideas will be accepted by whoever he's talking to at the time. Paul feels anxious if anybody disagrees with him, and would do anything to avoid an argument.

Then there's Bert, an engineer, who was once sold a set of children's encyclopaedias because he didn't want to upset the door-to-door salesman by saying 'No'. And Jennifer, an insurance clerk, who has a wardrobe full of clothes she never wears because she is too timid to withstand the barrage of persuasion directed at her by over-bearing saleswomen.

Admittedly this pattern of behaviour does have several short-term benefits. Initially, it will keep the other person happy, and often wealthier. You don't have to take responsibility for your own feelings, since you can always blame someone else; you tell yourself you feel annoyed because you have been 'badly treated', not because you chose to feel that way. You've convinced yourself you have no reason to change, because the problem didn't lie with you in the first place. When things are going well your friends and acquaintances may not see through you, so you can take pleasure from belonging to the 'in-crowd'.

Sadly, seeking approval in this way can only bring short-term rewards at the expense of long-term happiness. People learn they can't trust you because you're inconsistent. It is far better to stick firmly to your point of view, unless *you* find a good reason to change it. You cannot find security or happiness if you are beholden to other people's wishes, opinions and moods. Sooner or later they will begin to find you boring and unstimulating. Nobody likes having a yes-man around for long.

The most popular personalities are those with clearly defined and individual viewpoints. People are instinctively drawn to someone who has the strength of character to have a mind of her own.

Learn to agree to differ. You don't have to justify your opinions to anyone, so don't be afraid to express them. You may even find that people start coming to you for sound advice!

Look After Your Own Needs

One of the biggest fallacies of all is the belief that you should fulfil your obligations to others before doing anything for yourself.

Joan has spent her whole life running round after other people. As a girl she had to look after her cantankerous mother. She married a man who expected his wife to respond to his every whim, which she did. She had three children and devoted herself to them. Then her ageing mother had a stroke, and Joan cared for her twenty-four hours a day. She then had another child, and shortly after he had grown up and left home, her husband, who had retired, became ill and had to be nursed for the last few years of his life. Some time after he died, Joan met a man who suffered from a heart condition, giving her another opportunity to dedicate herself to looking after a sick and elderly person.

Often, people like Joan feel taken for granted and resentful. They wish they could be less unselfish, but somehow they don't seem to be able to say 'No'. What motivates them? The answer is there is something about their behaviour which gives them satisfaction, and changing seems too painful. What pleasure could they possibly get from being treated like that? Naturally, they feel useful and wanted, and pity, sympathy and martyrdom do have their payoffs. They attract attention and make them feel needed and appreciated.

The snag is that this sort of approval is not freely given to you for what you *are*. It is conditional on what you *do*. It is also addictive. You'll need more sympathy tomorrow than you did today just to keep yourself functioning, so you'll go to even greater lengths to place yourself at the disposal of other people. Eventually they'll see through your motives, so they'll be more and more reluctant to give you what you want, and might even lose their respect for you.

Escape From the Trap of Approval-Seeking Behaviour

It's simply not true that you must be accepted and approved of by everyone. Even your close friends and family will not approve of you all the time, and yet still love and accept you. So why should you worry about pleasing people you hardly know?

There is only one person whose approval you need, and that is *you*. It is nice to receive praise and admiration – it's all too rare in our competitive society – but the minute you allow it to dictate how you feel about yourself, you become like a rudderless boat at the mercy of the tides.

A serious problem arises if you have such a desperate need for approval that you give away your individuality, destroy your self-respect and hand over your power to live as you please. Psychologists recognize it as a sign of a deep-seated neurosis. Other people's opinions will only affect you if you have a poor self-image. As Eleanor Roosevelt so aptly put it, 'No one can make you feel inferior without your consent.' Don't give them permission.

> *The important thing is not what they think of me; it is what I think of them.*
>
> Queen Victoria

Escaping from the trap of approval-seeking behaviour is one of the biggest steps you can take towards building your self-esteem, but it rarely happens overnight; it is a gradual process that can be speeded up using our techniques. The important thing is to be always heading in the right direction.

Read the following sentence over and over again. Recite it to yourself when in Alpha Level until you have incorporated it into your unconscious thought patterns.

I *choose* how to react to others.

This simple truism will give you a whole new perspective, enabling you to deal with others' expectations, criticisms and, if it happens, their rejection of you. You will then be well on the way to genuine independence of thought, word and deed.

Don't Conform for the Sake of It . . .

In our culture we are expected to conform. From a very young age, we are rewarded for pleasing our parents, teachers and friends. We fall in line hoping to enjoy the pay-off – attention, praise, presents and so on. This becomes an unconscious habit which is difficult to shake off. If winning the approval of others is a measure of your self-esteem, you will allow others to make your decisions for you, dictate your opinions and choose how you will behave in their presence.

Once you have worked on your self-esteem, you can ask yourself 'What is it about me that makes others treat me as they do?' Our Dynamic Living Formula will provide the answer to this question. If you like the way others treat you, you will be satisfied with the answers you get, but if you think they treat you badly you may not. With a good self-image you will have the strength to decide for yourself whether to change the behaviour that others do not like. But it will be *your* decision, not theirs.

. . . Or Rebel

Deliberately rebelling is no more rewarding than conforming. In fact, it's a kind of 'conforming in reverse'. You are still not being true to yourself, and are still allowing others to dictate your actions, even if they are the opposite of what they want from you.

You can only achieve real freedom and healthy self-esteem by firmly deciding what you believe in and how you will conduct yourself, without being deflected by the whims of others.

> *What you think of me is none of my business.*
>
> Terry Cole-Whittaker

SUMMARY OF CHAPTER 9

1. Of all the relationships you will ever have, the one with yourself is the most important. You *must* learn to love and respect yourself.
2. Take care of your own love needs. You are lovable now, just as you are. It is impossible to love yourself too much, and real love is not conditional. This is not a selfish or egotistical philosophy – if you don't have love for yourself, how can you give any to others?
3. Self-esteem is not related to what you do. Do not allow 'failure' to dent your self-confidence. The only failure is giving up.
4. Don't dwell on your faults. This will only reinforce them.
5. Take responsibility for your values and opinions. Hold fast to them. Only change them if *you* choose to.
6. You choose how to react to others. Escape from the trap of approval-seeking behaviour and break away from their expectations. This is the road to your own personal power.

EXERCISE

Every day, when you go into Alpha Level, visualize yourself as you really want to be. Decide on your goals before relaxing. If you can't do this at first, it doesn't matter. Think about it, sense it, hear the sounds you associate with it. The longer and more vividly you can hold on to these images or impressions, the sooner they will come true.

10. The Dynamic Living Formula

The Dynamic Living Formula is a straightforward, easily remembered method of achieving whatever you want by re-directing your mental resources. It can be used to improve any area of your life. In fact, top sportspeople, entertainers and business executives all over the world are using it daily with great success.

We encourage you to use the 'Five A's', outlined below, for improving your self-image, and the Dynamic Living Formula, every day. Naturally they require practice and commitment, but you will find it gets easier as the days go by, so don't be discouraged if you don't get the hang of it in the first few sessions. Most people enjoy the peaceful, dreamy state known as 'Alpha', and the long-term benefits will make all your efforts worthwhile.

The Five A's

If you have done all the exercises in the preceding chapters, you will have a good idea of your level of self-esteem, self-image and self-confidence. You will know how to deal with any distressing incidents from the past which once upset you, and be able to draw upon good experiences to help you through any testing situations you are facing in the present.

Read and understand the Five A's: Awareness, Attitude, Acceptance, Action and Approval. Memorize them so you can recall them at will.

1. *Awareness*

What are your strengths and weaknesses? How do you relate to others? In which situations do you feel competent and comfortable? When do you feel uneasy or unable to cope? How do you feel about your physical make-up? Your intellectual abilities? Your emotional characteristics? Your way of dealing with social situations? How far apart is your real self-image from your ideal self-image?

Evaluate yourself as objectively as you can. It can be useful to discuss some aspects of yourself with a close friend, but remember that ultimately it is what *you* think that counts.

Once you know all this, you're on the way to doing something about it. Don't expect it to be an overnight process, though. It continues throughout your life but can (fortunately!) be speeded up by using our approach.

2. *Attitude*

Most of what you achieve in life is due to your attitude, not your intelligence or physical capabilities; if you have a poor self-image, it is because your attitude towards yourself needs to be changed. With the right attitude, you can succeed at almost anything.

Your attitude is nothing more than a collection of thoughts which can be changed, so choose to have a good attitude towards yourself. Decide that you're worth the effort of staying healthy, eating well, thinking happy thoughts, learning to relax and making your own choices.

Remember, right cause – right effect; right thinking – right action; right attitude – right result.

> *Take charge of your attitude. Don't let
> someone else choose it for you.*
>
> H. Jackson Brown Jnr

3. Acceptance

Acceptance does not mean deciding that you are what you are and nothing can be done about it. It is simply acknowledging to yourself, 'This is me, this is what I'm like, warts and all.' The secret of enjoying a good self-image is to learn to like yourself as you are, to improve what you can and accept that there are some things you cannot change. It doesn't mean telling yourself that other people can do things you cannot, and never will be able to do (which is nearly always untrue if your desire is strong enough).

Accepting what can't be changed – your height, your past, your sex, and so on – is necessary to a healthy self-image. Perfection is an unrealistic aim, and quite unnecessary for enjoying a healthy, happy and successful life. Accept and learn to love who you are, get away from the morbid preoccupation with your so-called faults, and start living instead.

4. Approval

Self-approval is having the strong belief that you are a person of value and you're doing your best. Every day, reassure yourself that you're a lovable and worthy person, moving in the right direction, making good progress towards your goal.

But don't be too impatient. Keep going. If you slip up, don't chastise yourself. Tell yourself you've made tremendous progress, you're getting where you want to be, and be proud of what you've achieved. Self-approval becomes a habit; one that is well worth acquiring.

5. Action

Now that you know where your strengths and weaknesses lie, have identified aspects of yourself which you can improve, accepted those that can't be changed, and decided to change your attitude, *take action*. If you need to lose weight, *do it*. If your attitude needs to change, *change it*. Every day, choose some little thing that you can do to build up your confidence, and put it into practice.

Allow *one hour a day* for working on yourself. This isn't very much for such a large return. Everyone has exactly the same amount of time every day, and most people waste at least an hour doing nothing in particular. Use the Dynamic Living Formula, listen to relaxation tapes twice a day to recondition your unconscious mind, read self-help books, listen to inspirational tapes and reward yourself for small successes along the way.

Don't forget, 'Beginning is half-done and half-won.' Make a start today.

The Dynamic Living Formula

Outlined below are the five basic principles of the Dynamic Living Formula. All five should be included in your hour-a-day routine, so that they become an integral part of your life.

1. Physical Relaxation

Physical relaxation has innumerable benefits: improved health and vitality; greater protection against stress and disease; more refreshing and satisfying sleep; increased self-confidence and heightened creativity. There isn't space to list them all here.

Relaxation does not just mean flopping down in front of the television, or enjoying a glass of wine while reading a book. This can, of course, be relaxing, but not to the same degree as deep relaxation, which allows the mind to drift down into

Alpha Level and access its intuitive powers. We can recharge our batteries and summon greater energy when required.

Find a quiet room to practise where you will not be disturbed. You should set aside twenty minutes or so. Sit or lie down, and make sure you are warm and comfortable, with your head and neck supported.

Now focus on your breathing, through your nose. Relaxation occurs as you breathe out, so as you exhale think the word 'relax' or 'calm', and be aware of your muscles and limbs going loose and flaccid. Do not hold your breath; this will increase tension. Try not to rush your relaxation sessions, and don't worry about whether you're 'doing it right' or not. Just focus on the feeling of letting go and allow it to happen – trying too hard may be counter-productive.

Deepen the sensation by slowly counting down from ten to one, or imagining yourself in a pleasant and comfortable place, such as a beach, a sheltered garden or a snug room in a country cottage.

At the end of the session, either allow yourself to drift down into natural sleep (if you are practising late at night), or sit quietly for a few minutes before getting up slowly and carrying on with your normal activities.

2. Mental Calmness

Mental calmness and physical relaxation are closely connected. When you are physically relaxed, your brain activity slows and you drift into Alpha Level. In this state, it is impossible to feel nervous tension. Your Left Brain quietens down, your Right Brain becomes more active and your unconscious mind becomes receptive to your affirmations and mental imagery.

Since the critical censor which controls the passage of ideas into your unconscious during the waking state is half asleep, it is vital to dwell only on positive, constructive thoughts. If distracting thoughts do occur, just repeat the word 'relax' to yourself until they float away.

3. *Visualization*

In Alpha state, you can use visualization to place positive thoughts in the form of pictures into your unconscious mind. It is as if you have a mental screen inside your head on which you can project the scenes and pictures you want. It is absolutely vital to see yourself as a successful person, brimming with self-confidence and enjoying a positive and healthy self-image. Visualization is the most powerful way of communicating your desires to your unconscious, so don't allow negative images to penetrate your mind.

If you find it difficult to visualize, don't worry. Although some people can actually 'see' things in their mind with crystal clarity, many cannot. If you are one of these, think, hear and feel the situation instead. It is just as effective. What really counts is being able to create and hold the impression, and feel good about it.

Focus on your potential, not the obstacles in your path. Once your unconscious is clear about what you want, it will find the solutions for you. Allowing your mind to be constantly full of thoughts about the negative aspects of your present situation rather than your desired outcome is a recipe for disaster.

Record over those old tapes that have been holding you back. See yourself acting as a confident person in situations you presently find difficult. Picture the house, the car, the garden you would like to own. Watch yourself making a great success of the work you would like to do. Build into yourself the qualities you desire and know that you need.

4. *Affirmations*

An affirmation is a statement you believe, or which you strongly desire to be true. They are at their most powerful when you are in Alpha Level. There are only three simple rules for using them effectively.

Firstly, always express them in the *present* tense. Not, 'I will be a confident person,' but 'I *am* a confident person.' Never, 'I will be a good public speaker,' but 'I *am* a good public speaker.' If you phrase your affirmations in the future tense, your unconscious will assume that they are not a priority at the moment. But it will start work immediately to make present-tense affirmations come true.

Secondly, phrase them in the *first* person. In other words, begin all your affirmations with, for example, '*I* am,' '*I* have,' or '*I* can.' Affirmations on behalf of others will not work. You cannot affirm, 'Jane loves me,' or 'Jim wants the same as I do.'

Thirdly, make sure your affirmations are expressed in the *positive*, never the negative. Your unconscious mind has diffi-culty telling the difference between a positive and a negative phrase, even if their meaning is the exact opposite. Affirming 'I am not fat,' might be interpreted as 'I am fat.' Say 'I am slim,' instead.

Your affirmations will be very effective if you recite them often during the day, and are extremely powerful if you say them in front of a mirror. The more you use them, the quicker you will progress. Write them out on a small card and carry them around in your pocket, or read them onto a cassette tape and play them over and over to yourself.

One valuable use of affirmations is to build up your desire to achieve your goal. Desire is a prerequisite for success; wanting something badly enough, and being willing to put the effort into having it, is the strongest motivator of all. Affirm to yourself, 'My strongest desire is to have high self-esteem. I yearn for an excellent self-image. I am determined to have plenty of self-confidence.'

A Selection of Affirmations for Strengthening Your Self-Image

Choose those which feel right for you, or compose your own, using the three basic guidelines:

- I like myself

- I love and approve of myself

- I am willing to release the past and live fully in the present

- It is safe for me to take charge of my own life
- I am willing to change and to grow
- I now release with ease all my old negative beliefs
- I forgive myself unconditionally
- I forgive my parents unconditionally
- I am loving, lovable and loved
- Every day in every way I am getting better and better
- I relax and allow my mind to be peaceful
- I automatically and joyfully focus on the positive
- I am enthusiastic about life and filled with energy and purpose
- I am perfect just as I am
- I am doing the best I can; I am at peace
- I am influenced only by positive thoughts and positive people
- My thinking is peaceful, calm and centred
- I trust my intuition to guide me in the right direction
- I am responsible for myself and my life
- I feel warm and loving toward myself
- I am worthy of all the good in my life
- I think, talk and act with confidence at all times
- I am at one with the Intelligence that created me; I am safe

Affirmations strengthen your desire for the qualities you want. With your mind full of healthy, positive thoughts, there is no room for negativity. Learn how to use them effectively.

5. The 'As If' Principle

If you act as if you are the kind of person you want to be, you will become that person. If you act confidently, you will become confident; if you act with courage, you will become courageous. You will find yourself handling difficult situations differently, and others will respond to you accordingly.

You can add power to the 'As If' Principle by deciding to act as if there is a Universal Intelligence caring for you. You may find this idea far-fetched, but it isn't really. It helps if you step back for a moment and think about who you are and where you came from.

Are you really just the result of DNA's incessant need to protect and reproduce itself, as some scientists would have us believe? Surely not! Every society in the world recognizes that there must be some Power overseeing us. Some call it God, or Krishna, or Allah. What would you call it? Does it have to have a name at all?

Now imagine the Intelligence that created you working tirelessly for you throughout your life, nourishing your body and mind and taking care of your spiritual needs. Wouldn't it be wonderful?

The universe is composed of matter and energy; we are all made up of matter, and we all have energy in varying degrees. A scientist once attempted to calculate the probability that the universe could be nothing more than the random arrangement of matter, and found the odds against it were so large most computers couldn't handle the figurework. The magnificent Intelligence that arranges everything must have been responsible for creating you, too. If so, it is most unlikely it would want to see you harmed; it would want to support and encourage you in every possible way.

Many great people have realized that this Universal Intelligence worked through them and that they owed their success to it. Thomas Edison was once asked where he got all his ideas from. 'I simply pluck them out of the air,' he replied. He knew his ability came from knowing how to access and use it to greater effect than the majority of us.

Yet even he had to cope with many experiences of failure before he tasted success. By the time he invented the incandescent light bulb, he had spent $40,000 (quite a sum in the 1870s) on many thousands of fruitless experiments. His resilience must have been tested to the full before he finally got it right, but, fortunately for us, he had the courage to keep trying.

For you to get the full benefit from the 'As If' Principle, you must *believe* that there is a Universal Intelligence. Once you have the feeling that something is taking care of you, you step out confidently, knowing that anything that happens is ultimately for your benefit. All you have to do is learn, like Thomas Edison, to have faith in yourself and the Intelligence that works through you.

Other Applications

Physical and mental relaxation, visualization, affirmations and the 'As If' Principle are the cornerstones of the Dynamic Living Formula, but they are not the whole story.

There are many other ways of using Alpha Level, some of which you have already come across in the exercises in previous chapters. Once you have mastered these powerful techniques, you will be able to apply them to any situations or goals that you set for yourself.

1. Reframing

The world around us does not influence and control our lives, but the meaning we attach to it does. A situation can look very different when seen through someone else's eyes. In other words, the interpretation of any event depends upon the 'frame' or context in which we perceive it. Reframing allows you to change your feelings and perceptions about an experience.

Imagine, for instance, that someone has made a rude remark and you feel angry and insulted. You could deal with this by asking yourself questions which lead you to alternative views of the situation. 'Was he talking to someone other than me?' 'Did he really mean what he said?' 'Is he feeling angry with himself?' 'Is he having a bad day?' 'What other meanings could there be?' Very soon, the remark loses its significance.

Be quite clear on one point: reframing is not a way of fooling yourself into believing that everything in the garden is coming up roses; rather it is a method of finding alternative ways of viewing a situation so that you can deal with it more effectively.

> *There is nothing either good or bad,*
> *but thinking makes it so.*
>
> William Shakespeare

We suggest two ways in which reframing can help you raise your self-esteem.

Firstly, if your mind is dwelling on an event from the past, go into Alpha and reframe it. If you had a major disappointment, reframe it by looking for its positive side. Every situation, however bleak at the time, has its compensations, even if they only become apparent with the benefit of hindsight.

Perhaps you once received poor service in a restaurant, but were too timid to complain. See yourself putting your viewpoint across assertively, and getting the results you would have liked. Or you stayed at home watching television, full of disappointment and hurt, because a friend chose to go out with somebody else rather than spend time with you. Sense yourself feeling happy that you had a relaxing evening on your own recharging your batteries.

Secondly, review the events of the day in your mind every evening just before you drift off to sleep. If anything happened which left you feeling less than completely satisfied, see it working out as you would have wished.

Use questions to discover the positive angle of any situation:

'What else could this mean?'
'What positive value does this have?'
'What have I learnt that will benefit me in the future?'
'How does it help me in the wider scheme of things?'

2. Anchoring

Anchoring is a way of drawing on your past experiences to help you cope better with present and future situations. It works by enabling you to re-experience the confident and positive feelings you associated with the past event.

Many top sportspeople use anchors all the time. The tennis player who bounces the ball repeatedly before serving, the footballer who clenches his fist before taking a penalty, and the batsman who prods the pitch with his bat between deliveries, are all using them to centre themselves and recreate that winning feeling before they go into action.

To use an anchor you have to, first of all, generate in yourself the particular set of feelings you want to use, and then find a way of bringing these forth at will. Imagine you have been asked to give a talk to a large audience, and you are feeling apprehensive about addressing so many people. Perhaps you once spoke to a small group of people at a wedding, or talked about a hobby at your children's school. Suppose your talk was well received, you felt good about doing it and enjoyed the compliments that came your way. Go into Alpha and relive that event in as much detail as you can. Recall all the sights, sounds, smells and feelings. Draw on all your powers of imagination so that you picture it as vividly as possible. Then 'anchor' those feelings by choosing a gesture that you wouldn't normally use, such as putting the thumb and fingers of one hand together, tugging your ear lobe or clenching your fist. You can also mutter a short phrase, such as 'Anchor' or 'Calm', to accentuate the feeling.

Now project your mind into the future. There you are, in your imagination, about to give your speech. See yourself activating the anchor by using the specific gesture, and feel a surge of positive emotion overwhelming you. Visualize your-self giving the talk – at ease, speaking confidently, receiving the applause of the audience, happy and successful.

When the day of the talk arrives, activate the anchor again just before you take your place at the speaker's rostrum. Those feelings of relaxed self-assurance and courage will give you all the confidence and poise you need.

Anchoring is a tried and tested technique which may appear far-fetched at first, but is one of the most powerful weapons in your armoury. Remember, you will get no benefit at all from just reading about it. Try it! After a few attempts, you will be amazed how strongly you can summon up positive feelings at will and use them to bolster your confidence.

3. Changing the Balance of Pleasure and Pain

Our lives are governed by the pleasure and pain that we believe will result from our actions. We (usually unknowingly) ask ourselves, 'If I go ahead with this course of action, how much pleasure will it bring? How much pain? If I do not go ahead, how much pleasure will I forego? How much pain will I avoid?'

Every decision we take is a result of weighing up the pleasure–pain balance. On a hot day, we may eat an ice-cream, anticipating the short-term pleasure of that cool, creamy taste, but knowing that the long-term consequences are harm to our bodies from excess calories and too much sugar and fat. We all know instances where we have chosen to forego long-term benefits because of the short-term effort and discomfort.

An athlete, for example, knows that training is hard work, time-consuming and occasionally painful, but is willing to endure the discomfort because the long-term payoffs are so attractive. If she pictures herself crossing the winning line to rapturous applause, and having the medal placed round her neck, she will happily put in the time and effort required to reach that goal.

You, too, can use the pleasure–pain principle to engineer the circumstances you want. Imagine the pleasure you will get from having a strong self-image and loads of confidence. Use mental imagery and affirmations to crystallize that feeling. Now conjure up the pain of having low self-esteem. See yourself being walked all over by others, afraid to speak up for yourself, always settling for second best. Feel the embarrassment, the frustration, the lack of self-respect. When you can hold both the pleasure of your success in your mind, and the pain of not achieving it, your unconscious and entire nervous system will set about making your chosen course a reality.

You now have the basic toolkit to enable you to recondition your mind for a genuine feeling of self-worth and confidence in everything you do. But you know a hammer can't bang in a nail unless you take it out of the toolbox. Similarly, reading a book will leave you with an inspirational warm feeling, but do absolutely nothing for your self-esteem unless you practise the exercises and apply the techniques for yourself.

SUMMARY OF CHAPTER 10

1. The Dynamic Living Formula can be used to improve any aspect of your life, and is especially effective at raising self-esteem. It requires practice and commitment, but most people soon get the hang of it and notice the benefits for themselves.
2. The Five A's – Awareness, Attitude, Acceptance, Approval and Action – provide an easily remembered system for focussing on improving your self-image and confidence.
3. Physical relaxation and mental calmness are the keys to unlocking the capabilities of your Right Brain. Once you have mastered these skills, your affirmations and visualizations will be much more effective. You can also use reframing and anchoring to deal with specific problems and opportunities.
4. Use the 'As If' Principle to change your beliefs. Act as if you are confident, and you will become confident. Act as if the Universal Intelligence is supporting you and you will have greater self-assurance and peace of mind.
5. All these techniques can be used to mentally alter the balance of pleasure and pain you associate with your actions. Your progress toward your goal will then become irresistible.

11. Twelve More Steps To High Self-Esteem

You now know how to access your unconscious and make the changes you desire, but we realize it's not always convenient to go into Alpha when you need an instant boost of confidence. We have to work at building confidence continually, and in this chapter we offer you a wealth of things you can do at any time. If you practise them, they build into a comprehensive programme for success. You will feel and act like a new person, notice others treating you with greater respect, and, more importantly, have more self-respect too.

> *You cannot dream yourself a character;*
> *you must hammer and forge*
> *yourself one.*
>
> James A. Froude

1. See Yourself As Confident and Successful

If you want to be successful, you must 'see' yourself succeeding. No ifs or buts. If you envisage yourself as a failure, you will be one. Your mind will act on the pictures and thoughts it receives and bring about whatever you imagine.

Golfers spend many hours seeing themselves hit the perfect shot. Entertainers consciously dream about that magic moment when they hold the audience in the palm of their hand. When such positive images are impressed firmly enough on the unconscious, you expect to succeed; and once you expect to succeed – you do!

2. Listen to Your Self-Talk – and Correct It!

How you talk to yourself is very important. If your self-talk is positive, inspiring and enthusiastic, you will become a positive, inspiring and enthusiastic person. If you are always dwelling on the negative, running yourself down, criticizing others and finding the black side of every situation, it will be impossible to improve your self-esteem.

Listen to your internal dialogue and take firm control! Be constantly on your guard; use 'thought stopping' whenever you become aware of a damaging thought, and replace it with a constructive one.

3. Take Responsibility

You now know that nobody else can build your self-respect, make you feel confident or create a good self-image for you. Only you can do these things. Many find change threatening, and you will discover that some people who are close to you will not know how to cope with your new-found confidence. They may even attempt to put you back in your place, but don't be fooled; they are *not* trying to help you. They're trying to deal with their resentment of your happiness and success.

Taking responsibility means making a firm commitment to setting goals, planning your strategy and taking action. If *you* don't do it, who will? Don't allow anyone to deflect you from your chosen course.

4. Build On Your Strengths

If you are going to break the Spiral of Despair you must focus on your potential, not your limitations. Many people feel they are not as clever, athletic or good-looking as others. Every time they compare themselves, it makes them feel inferior. There is nothing more likely to undermine your self-confidence, so stop doing it!

You probably haven't given much in-depth thought to your own strengths before. Are you a good communicator who gets on well with other people? Are you instinctively kind and helpful to others? Do you make a good and sympathetic listener? These are valuable qualities that many people don't have. Work out a strategy for using all your strengths to the full.

There is no room for self-doubt and self-criticism in a mind continually kept full of optimism and positive thoughts.

5. Concentrate on What You Do Well

The world is full of unsuccessful people who have talent. Even if they are aware of their natural aptitude, they may not have the confidence or tenacity to develop their skills. They feel that, no matter how good they are, someone else is bound to be better.

Focus your mind on the things you know you do well. Perhaps you can bake delicious cakes, paint, write, or have 'green fingers'. If so, make cakes for your friends and neighbours (you will be rewarded many times over for the effort involved by their appreciation). Display your paintings around the house to remind yourself of your prowess. Send some of your stories to magazines for publication. Arrange your plants inside and outside your home.

If you worry about something you are not so good at, ask yourself 'Does it really matter?' If it's something you don't even enjoy, it could be that your parents and teachers discouraged you. Unless it's important to you now, it's totally irrelevant.

It is not usually natural talent and ability which makes the difference, but confidence and persistence, so devote yourself to something you do well. You'll find yourself happily taking on progressively more difficult challenges. Use the Dynamic Living Formula to visualize your success. You don't have to become Picasso or Agatha Christie overnight to enjoy and appreciate what you can accomplish right now.

6. Stop Being What Others Want You To Be

Once you learn to stop doing things just because others expect it, the sense of freedom can be exhilarating. If you are true to your instincts, you will find your real identity. You will discover your own individual way of being, the contribution you can make that is yours and yours alone.

If you feel you are always having to pretend to be something you are not, or if an activity doesn't feel right, ask yourself, 'Why am I doing this? Do I really want to, or is it simply because somebody else expects it? What benefits do I get from fooling myself in this way?' Then decide how you would like to be, and what you would rather be doing, and do that instead.

7. Write Down Your Goals

One reason most people don't achieve very much in life is that they don't really know what they want. If you don't know where you want to get to, how will you know which direction to move in or recognize when you've arrived?

Setting goals for yourself is the most powerful way of motivating yourself for success. Writing them down adds to their power; every time you commit them to paper, your unconscious mind takes notice, then sets about helping you achieve them.

Update your list every two or three months and monitor your progress; include a brief statement of how you intend to achieve each goal. If you feel you are not getting anywhere, don't abandon the goal; think carefully about where you are going wrong, go into Alpha and ask your unconscious to assist, and then change direction.

People who have followed this advice are easy to spot: they are almost always happy, well-balanced and very successful. Join them!

8. Modelling

We all know people who seem to have some, if not all, of the qualities we want for ourselves. We admire them and wish we could be like them, but we know that this isn't enough; we have to *do* something.

You can save years of effort by using a technique called 'modelling'. The idea is very simple. Decide what qualities you want, find someone who already has them, then watch, listen and learn how he does it.

You can observe his behaviour, but if this isn't enough, *ask* him how it feels to behave in that way, and what thoughts he has at the time. He will probably be very flattered, and more than willing to share his secrets! Adopt these thought patterns for yourself. Once you know what to do, practise, practise, practise.

Find out what it feels like to be really proud of yourself. Decide what you have to think and believe to raise your self-esteem, and then do it. Go into Alpha and affirm, visualize and anchor your way to self-assurance and ever-growing confidence.

9. Forgive Your Parents

This is a very important step, because you can't throw away a heavy burden of resentment which is holding you back until you forgive your parents unconditionally. Even if they did the most dreadful things to you when you were a child, realize that dwelling on it is only causing *you* pain. Even if they apologized, you could still not change those unhappy events.

Use reframing to change your feelings about such events. The past is dead, *but you're not*. Resolve to live in the present.

10. Surround Yourself With Supportive Friends

The company you keep is all-important. Negative, critical people will make it harder for you to become positive and accepting, and you should avoid them; you won't change them. They can only decide to change for themselves. Don't let them drag you down.

Finding supportive friends does not necessarily mean meeting new people; it is probably more rewarding to deepen your relationships with your existing circle. Share your feelings more openly; don't be afraid to be vulnerable. Ask them to point out any negativity which is creeping into your conversation. Tell them you're letting go of the past, and suggest they help you by talking about the present and future. Tell them what you are hoping to achieve and ask for their support.

A friend is someone who wants the best for you, so be wary of anyone who reacts by mocking or criticizing you. That's exactly the sort of company you need to avoid.

11. Take Care of the Child Within

The child you once were did not disappear when you reached that magical age of adulthood. She lives on inside you, and you can overlook her if you wish, but she will find a way of making her presence felt. Forget her at your peril!

Many psychotherapists see the inner child as the root cause of much adult unhappiness. This child may still be carrying all the guilt experienced so many years ago. An unhappy child is not likely to grow into a happy adult unless the anger and resentment can be resolved. Here are some ways of releasing the pain.

Tell your inner child you would like to talk to her. Tell her you love her and will take care of her. Ask what you can do to make her happy. Do those silly things that your child enjoys.

Use visualizations when in Alpha. Here is a very powerful one. Imagine you are walking through a park when you see a little child approaching you. You recognize her as yourself, at six years old. You allow her to sit on your knee, and you talk to her. Listen carefully to what she is saying. What would you like to say to her? Promise to look after her and love her from now on.

Get hold of a photograph of yourself when you were small, and put it somewhere where you will see it every day. Smile and acknowledge it.

It is amazing how many people are ashamed of the child they once were. It helps if you realize that you had very little control over your circumstances then; you did the best you could with the knowledge you had at the time. You've come a long way since then. Be proud of what you are, and caring and sympathetic towards that very special little person.

12. Persist Until You Succeed

Changing your attitude to yourself will take time: if you have had a poor self-image for thirty years, don't expect to change it overnight. But take heart! It only takes thirty days to lay the foundations for a lasting change in your thinking habits, and hence in your actions and your life.

Never give up. Take charge of your thinking, see yourself in action and note the changes that are taking place. Each small victory will add to your progress, so compliment yourself as you approach your goal. See it as an exciting, life-long adventure and, above all, enjoy it.

SUMMARY OF CHAPTER 11

Chapter 11 gives you many ideas that you can put into practice immediately, to add to the other exercises in this book. Many of them involve writing things down: we've asked you to make lists of your strengths and weaknesses, complete sentences, construct affirmations, think about your goals and so on.

Why not buy yourself a small notebook and keep them all together? Call it your 'personal growth diary', or whatever name you think best. Jot down your Alpha experiences, including the feelings generated by reframing exercises, successful uses of the anchoring technique and all the other positive steps you take.

Update it regularly, express your thoughts and feelings in it, and use it to monitor your personal growth. Date every entry, and spend a few minutes each day skimming through it. As you see all the progress you are making, you'll feel really good about yourself, and have plenty of assurance that your life is beginning to head in the right direction.

12. Building The Self-Esteem Of Others

Nathan, a sales executive for a leading company, was discussing with his colleagues people who had made a difference in their lives. He mentioned a teacher who had first inspired his love of English literature at school, and wondered what had become of her. Someone suggested that he try to contact her, so he wrote to his old school asking for her address.

It turned out that she had retired some twenty years ago, but Nathan eventually located her in a retirement home. He wrote a long letter expressing his appreciation, and telling her of all the enjoyment he had derived from reading the classics over the years.

After a few weeks, she wrote to him. She said she had not had any contact at all with either the school or any of her former pupils since she retired. She often felt that her life had been wasted, since no one had ever given her any acknowledgement, but Nathan's letter had made all the difference; it made her feel as if her career and her life had been worthwhile.

Nathan read the letter to his colleagues. They were all so touched that they agreed to write to at least one person every week to express their gratitude for what that person had done.

Every kind, sincere act of this nature makes us feel good about ourselves. The world would be a depressing place if it were possible to further our own growth by destroying someone else! Every time we do or say something to raise the self-esteem of others we simultaneously improve our own self-image to at least the same degree.

As we've said, nearly everyone we meet has lower self-esteem than they could have. Anything we can do to raise the self-esteem of another person not only improves the quality of her life, but also improves our personal relationships, and ultimately reflects back to us. It is simply not possible to build ourselves up by knocking others down.

From time immemorial, folk stories have told of the villain who bullies and double-crosses others for his own gain, and who eventually gets his come-uppance. Nowadays, we see modern villains climbing the ladder of material success on the backs of those who they have trodden on. Many end up in early graves, destroyed by the very stress they have created.

The secret of making others feel valued is never to say or do anything that causes them to feel inadequate, and to take every opportunity to bolster their self-confidence. A good guideline is: 'Do unto others as you would be done by.' You can have a far greater impact on them than you would imagine, and a caring attitude can help overcome seemingly insoluble problems.

The founder of 'Person-Centred Counselling', Carl Rogers, knew more than most about building others' self-esteem. He maintained that you would automatically assist a person in his spiritual and psychological development if you observed three straightforward ground rules. His system of therapy is the most widely used in the Western world.

His first rule was to offer unconditional positive approval and total acceptance of the other. No judging, criticizing or sarcasm, and certainly no mocking or moralizing. He showed how the other person will always feel respected and worthy if you can freely convey an attitude of unreserved caring and support.

Secondly, he stressed the vital importance of empathy, the ability to sense what the other is feeling, and understand her perception of the world. This is not easy; it requires a level of careful listening, patience and sensitivity which the average person finds very demanding.

Thirdly, you must be genuine, or 'congruent'. You must always be yourself in any interaction; if not, how can you help somebody else to be himself? Good relationships can only be formed if both parties are willing to share their real feelings.

Rogers claimed that a counsellor capable of expressing these qualities could help a person through a range of psychological disturbances, from mild neurosis to deep-seated anxiety and depression, without any further specialist knowledge of the actual condition.

So what can you do to develop a genuine caring attitude towards others, and help strengthen their feelings of self-worth every time you get the opportunity? We would like to suggest eight ways of putting this into practice.

1. Give Them Your Attention

Everyone knows we pay attention to people and things we consider important, and ignore whoever and whatever we do not. If someone is talking to us and we give the impression we're not listening, it conveys the message, 'I don't regard you as valuable and important enough to distract me from what I'm doing.' A person with a good feeling of self-worth will simply tell himself that you are preoccupied and move on to something else, but, sadly, someone with low self-esteem will interpret it as further proof he's not worth very much.

When you are talking to someone who is shuffling papers or fidgeting, you feel ill-at-ease and offended, so don't treat others in this way. The best thing is to look him in the eye, drop what you're doing and just listen. Remember, we all have two ears and one mouth, and this is roughly the right proportion to use them in!

2. Show Your Appreciation and Gratitude

This is so simple, yet effective. Say 'Thank you', even if someone has only done what was expected of him. If he has done you a special favour or shown kindness, buy him a small present or card to make him feel appreciated and worthwhile. You don't have to make a big fuss, or engage in an elaborate ritual. Just reinforcing your words with a smile or a warm handshake adds conviction without being over-effusive.

3. Never Criticize or Ridicule

Thoughtless criticism is a very effective way of destroying another's self-confidence. We all do the best we can most of the time, and it hurts when somebody belittles our efforts. Criticism makes us feel angry and resentful; it rarely inspires us to greater efforts.

There are, of course, times when we genuinely feel let down, when we want to point out that something could have been done better; but don't confuse an inferior standard of work or an indifferent performance with the value of the person. Say, 'You could have done this better if you had used this method,' not 'You are a stupid, careless person.' In this way you get your point across while leaving his self-regard intact.

Above all, don't be judgemental and don't moralize. His moral standards may be different to yours, so don't impose your values on him. You won't increase his self-respect by trying to make him feel guilty. Everyone has their own reasons for the way they behave, so don't presume the right to criticize because you don't ever have all the facts.

Sarcasm is another form of communication which belittles, as well as making the speaker sound contemptuous and abrasive and the receiver feel embarrassed. Never, ever use sarcasm with children. They often do not understand what you are really trying to say, and feel humiliated and confused.

You can make a dramatic improvement in your self-esteem by deliberately avoiding sarcasm and refusing to criticize anyone. Once you've mastered this, it feels as if a great burden has been lifted from your shoulders.

4. Listen Attentively

Nothing communicates acceptance and empathy as much as a sympathetic ear. It builds trust, and shows someone that you value him enough to spend time with him.

Real listening is making the effort to really grasp what someone says, and communicating your understanding to him.

Not listening is the greatest disrespect you can show another. It is even more important to listen carefully if the speaker is a young person, or someone who differs ethnically or racially from yourself.

There are some simple rules for good listening which, like any other skill, improves with practice. The first is to realize that listening is usually all the other person requires of you. If he's telling you about his troubles, it's not because he's looking for clever or instant solutions, or good advice. Your attention is often enough to make him feel much better. If he is in pain, silently project loving, caring thoughts towards him, and express your conviction that things will improve.

This doesn't mean that you have to agree with what he's saying. It's perfectly alright to accept another's feelings without sharing them. If you disagree, tell him you hear what he says, but you would take a different view. Make the best use of body language, by leaning forward and facing the person squarely.

Your first impression of what someone has said may not be accurate, so every so often confirm that you've listened to what he's told you by giving feedback. Précis what he's said and play it back to him. Say, 'What I understand you to be saying is . . .,' or 'How do you mean?', or any phrase you're comfortable with. If you've misheard or misunderstood him, he'll correct you, which will build up mutual trust.

Make sure that you don't give the impression that you're just waiting for a pause so you can jump in. The mind can absorb three times as much information per minute than the average person can speak, so it is very tempting to work out your reply and rehearse it before the other has finished what he's saying. A conversation was once described as two people each waiting for the other to stop speaking so that they can start talking!

Try counting to three after the other has stopped before beginning your reply. This allows you to concentrate better, make sure he really has finished, and demonstrate your respect for him.

5. Show Your Acceptance and Approval

Character faults and 'bad' behaviour often melt away if not commented on by other people. Making an issue of something gives it strength, so get into the habit of praising the good and ignoring the bad.

Don't put on an insincere show of flattery. Simply pinpoint the person's genuine strengths and then voice your approval. This will make her feel accepted and appreciated, and selective praise will eventually bring out the best in anybody. If she puts herself down, don't agree or disagree with her. Some people say disparaging things about themselves knowing that they're not true, hoping to manipulate you into paying them compliments. Be aware of this and don't fall for it.

Finally, one of the easiest and most effective ways of showing someone you approve of her is to smile. A warm smile says more than words ever could; and when you smile on the outside, you smile on the inside too. Your face lights up, your body relaxes and you actually feel much happier within yourself.

6. Express Your Admiration

We can always find something to admire in another: kindness, honesty, generosity, determination, sporting prowess and so on. We can give pleasure by noticing prized possessions, such as a painting, piece of furniture or an item of clothing. Pick out something that obviously means a lot to them, or compliment their appearance or dress sense.

Work towards making the other person feel that he is more valuable, and is capable of doing much more than he thinks he is. This is more than mere encouragement. If you can plant the seed of a suggestion in his mind that he *can* achieve something new, *can* make a success of something, it could grow. You may help to make that one dream come true, and could also contribute to transforming his whole life. Bringing out someone else's potential can be just as exciting and rewarding as bringing out your own!

Look for their good points – and let them know you're aware of them. They may not realize that you appreciate their strengths, and would be gratified to learn that you do. If someone feels valued and understood in your presence, they'll enjoy being with you and feel safe to disclose more of themselves. This is the basis of deep, long-lasting personal relationships.

7. Use Open-Ended Questions

An open-ended question is the opposite to a closed question, which invites a 'Yes', 'No' or 'Don't know' response. 'Are you feeling happy?' demands a yes or no answer. It is a conversation killer. Having said yes or no, the speaker can clam up, knowing that your expectations have been met.

Now think about the question, 'Why do you look so happy today?' You cannot simply reply 'Yes' or 'No' because you haven't answered the question; you must give a much fuller response. Open-ended questions allow another to speak freely for however long or little as they wish, and give him the confidence to continue the conversation. Avoiding closed questions is a useful skill for building rapport with others.

> *I have six honest serving men*
> *Who taught me all I know.*
> *Their names are what and where and*
> *when*
> *And which and why and how.*
>
> Rudyard Kipling

8. Never Argue

If you have respect for yourself and confidence in your opinions, you will not be unduly worried if others do not agree with you, and you will be able to accept their views in the same spirit. So don't argue if you can help it. Arguing disrupts the conversation, raises the temperature and can ultimately destroy friendships and working relationships. Moreover, it doesn't change anybody's opinion. 'A man convinced against his will,' goes the old saying, 'is of the same opinion still.'

It is self-defeating to allow yourself to get into a heated argument, since you will ultimately lose friends. We know of someone with very sincere views on a wide range of issues who never misses an opportunity to bombard us with his attitude to injustice the world over. He takes pride in winning every argument, and everyone recognizes that he knows his subject and debates with passion and logic. However, he hasn't noticed that groups enjoying light-hearted banter at social gatherings will evaporate as he approaches, fearful that the discussion will degenerate into a sermon or a slanging match.

If someone says something you feel you have to take issue with, the best way forward is to invent a third party to argue your point for you. This way, the debate doesn't become personal. Say 'Yes, I agree with that point, but what would you say to someone who said . . .'

Keen debaters may find others avoiding them, and must learn to admit they might sometimes be wrong if they want to stay accepted as part of a social group. You will be much happier if you decide to refuse to argue at all. Instead, make a conscious effort to help others to build up their self-esteem – and then sit back and enjoy the rewards!

Always remember that whatever you say or do to help or hinder someone will eventually rebound on you directly or indirectly. Making someone feel good about himself is just about the highest service you can render; it is worth practising until it becomes a habit.

If you find it difficult to start with, try practising at home with your children and partner. It certainly won't do your domestic life any harm. Explain what you are doing and encourage them to join in. Before long you will find you are playing a new style of 'happy families' which will stand all of you in very good stead for the future.

SUMMARY OF CHAPTER 12

1. Anything we can do to help other people have more positive feelings about themselves will rebound on our own self-regard. Show others your approval of them, try and sense what they are feeling, and be genuine in your concern.
2. We list eight ways in which you can build others' self-esteem. Some of them are easy to do immediately, others take a little practice. The effort you make will repay you many times over as others warm to you and make you feel better about yourself too.
3. Start with people you know well. As your confidence grows, it will become second nature to you. Watch your circle of friends grow!

13. A Thirty-Day Programme For Developing Your Self-Esteem

It takes twenty-eight days to change a habit, so we've divided our self-esteem training programme into four weeks plus two extra days for good measure. If you have our cassette tape 'Relax and Build Your Self-Esteem' you will find it easy to relax and use visualization and affirmations. Devote an hour a day to this programme – two twenty-minute relaxation sessions and another twenty minutes either reading this book, or listening to our instructional tape 'Creating Confidence – The Secrets of Self-Esteem'. Do the practical exercises every day for thirty days, then on a regular basis.

We have set out details of twelve exercises, three to be done per week. You will recognize most of them as being a summary of those listed at the end of each chapter. Most can be done in a spare moment, or without interrupting other activities. They will help you to make progress by altering your conscious thinking and reconditioning the unconscious thought patterns which need to be changed.

Week 1

Exercise 1

Concentrate on becoming more objectively aware of yourself. Every so often, take stock of how you are feeling. Be aware of the thoughts in your head; censor any negative internal dialogue and change it to positive, using 'thought stopping'. If someone or some situation is putting you under pressure and you feel you're not coping, affirm that you're in charge and that nothing and no one can put you down unless you allow them to.

If this sounds like quite a challenge, don't worry. The more practice you get, the easier it becomes, and before too long, it will be part of you. The important thing is that you are determined to succeed. As long as you head in the right direction and keep going, you will get there.

Exercise 2

Use affirmations to recondition your unconscious mind by feeding in positive thoughts about yourself every day. Choose ones which you feel are appropriate, or make up your own. If there is no specific aspect you wish to work on, start with, 'I like myself,' 'I feel good about myself,' or 'Every day, in every way, I'm getting more and more confident.'

You will find it helps to write your affirmations on a small card and carry it around with you, or record them onto a cassette tape and play it just before going to sleep and as you wake up. Repeating them in front of a mirror also adds to their power.

Exercise 3

Write down at least two or three of your positive attributes every day. You'll have a list of about twenty by the end of the week. Don't worry if they appear trivial; it's possible you are unaware of their importance to yourself and others. For instance, if you have a pleasant smile and a cheery turn of phrase you may be giving lots of pleasure to people without realizing it.

Make as long a list as you can. These are the strengths on which you can and must build.

Week 2

Exercise 1

Every morning before getting up, focus your attention on the way you really want your day to go. Visualize or imagine yourself acting as the kind of person you would like to be. Hold this ideal in your mind throughout the day. Don't worry if you can't see a clear picture in your mind's eye; many of us find it difficult and feel more comfortable hearing or feeling things.

If you can visualize or imagine your day unfolding precisely as you wish and hold it in your mind, events are far more likely to come up to your expectations.

Exercise 2

Every evening, run through all the events of the day in your mind. Imagine those that didn't work out happening as you would have liked them to. This will help you to think of the day in a more positive light, prepare you to handle the following day even better, and will boost your self-image and confidence.

Exercise 3

Write down your negative qualities, cross them out and replace them with their positive equivalents. Then focus on the positives. List them, and add them to your affirmations in the form 'I am . . . .'. Record them onto your cassette tape and repeat them to yourself at frequent intervals.

Remember, what you think of as your negative qualities are merely learned responses, programmed into you in the past. You can wipe out the misconceptions and see them for what they really are – illusions that can be changed. Focusing on the positive will slowly and surely build the desired qualities into your psyche.

Week 3

Exercise 1

Each day, tackle one little thing that requires you to gather up your courage. Building confidence is all about taking small steps, so make this a habit. Don't forget that confidence is something you *do*, not something that happens to you or something you have. Every day you try something new, you become a little more self-assured.

Exercise 2

Help to raise the self-esteem of three other people every day. Start with those closest to you – your family, friends and work colleagues – until you feel comfortable doing it for complete strangers. A kind word, an unsolicited compliment, a spontaneous smile, a positive remark – they cost so little and bring so much benefit to the recipient. They'll respond to you with warmth and gratitude, and this will automatically make you feel a lot better about yourself.

If you help three people a day, within a year you'll have brought pleasure and encouragement to a thousand, and can enjoy the satisfaction of knowing that you're building your self-esteem at the same time.

Exercise 3

Practise being more assertive. When someone is putting pressure on you or irritating you, calmly say what you feel. If they're trying to get you to do something you'd rather not, or attempting to force you to go along with something you don't want to, say 'No' firmly. Don't allow anyone to take advantage of you.

If you fail in this, you will simply create more problems by subjecting yourself to needless pressure, harming your self-image and raising your stress level. Save yourself a lot of trouble in the future by learning how to be more assertive and putting your new-found skills into practice.

Week 4

Exercise 1

Use the 'Reframing' technique described in Chapter 10. Re-run events from the past that are still troubling you; they need to be dealt with. When you are in Alpha Level, your unconscious mind knows exactly what is right for you at that moment.

Exercise 2

Practise using the 'Anchoring' technique daily (see Chapter 10). You'll find it gets easier and easier, and the benefits will become clear as each new success builds upon previous victories.

Exercise 3

Incorporate the 'As If' principle into your life; live as if you have within and around you a Power that is guiding and supporting you, constantly nourishing your mind and body, giving you all the confidence you need. Live securely in the knowledge that everything ultimately works out for your benefit. You'll find that life takes on a whole new meaning.

It is important to integrate these exercises into your daily life if you really want to affect lasting changes. Remember, there is no such thing as failure, only giving up too soon. Practice makes permanent. If you practise negative thinking and behave as if you have no confidence, that too will become permanent. You have it within your grasp to create health, happiness and success in whatever form you desire. Go for it!

14. The New You

Congratulations on reaching the last chapter! We hope you've enjoyed reading this book, and have decided to make some changes in your life. You will feel much more positively about yourself once you've worked through all the exercises, learned to relax more deeply and think more constructively, and discovered how rewarding it can be to help others feel better about themselves. You will be poised for a life of happiness and success.

What do you think it is about people with high self-esteem that makes them so successful? What enables them to take full advantage of life's opportunities and attract the right people into their lives?

Psychologists have spent years studying this. They have found that a good self-image has many spin-offs, including some unexpected ones. Did you know, for example, that physical changes take place as self-confidence increases? Your sense of humour is also sharpened and, although you feel less bound by the opinions of others, you are likely to make a much greater contribution to society in general and to the people in your close circle.

All of us have the capacity to grow mentally, emotionally and spiritually. It's not a question of whether you *can*, but whether your desire and sense of commitment are strong enough. We all have untapped reserves of energy, joy and enthusiasm, but it takes more than reading an inspirational book or listening to a tape to make a meaningful difference in your life. You need to invest some time, and be prepared to give it your very best shot.

You will find it well worth your while. Soon you will begin to feel better about yourself as your life starts to improve. The gains will quickly gather pace, and with a little effort every day, you'll soon be moving in the right direction; one year from now you'll feel like a whole new person.

The most crucial judgement you'll ever make is the one about yourself. And when you've created a better self-image, you'll judge yourself by your own standards, not somebody else's. You'll know if you're living up to your own expectations, or doing things just because it is expected of you.

You won't put unnecessary pressure on yourself by thinking you have to do everything well and never make mistakes. Once the fear of failure is removed, you'll be more open to new ideas, more inventive, more creative than ever before. You'll be more willing to move out of your comfort zone and take risks. Procrastination will be a thing of the past. You'll realize that great truth: you can get whatever you want out of life if you are adventurous enough and willing to invest the time and effort.

Since self-esteem is basically how you feel about yourself, you'll feel more loved than ever before, because you are taking care of your own love needs. Every day you'll affirm that you're loving, lovable and loved. You'll tell yourself you like yourself, over and over again. You'll savour the sense of belongingness and emotional security this brings.

You'll take responsibility for yourself and your actions – no more seeking to blame circumstances and other people when you find yourself in difficulties. Creating the link in your mind between cause and effect will encourage you to be more self-sufficient and more motivated in heading towards your goals.

You know that there are no guarantees in life, and if you're not getting what you want it's because you're going about it the wrong way. Most successful people create their own luck with foresight and perseverance. Your life will become an adventure with a difference; you'll realize that you cannot fail as long as you keep moving in the right direction.

> *People tell me I'm lucky, but I've noticed*
> *the harder I practise, the luckier I get.*
>
> Gary Player

Your physical features will alter. People will ask what you've done, expecting you to say that you've changed your hairstyle or work out regularly at a gym. Your whole body will become more relaxed. Your face, cheeks, mouth, and jaw will look and feel less tense; the tightness around your eyes and head will melt away; your posture straightens and improves. Your whole appearance will radiate confidence and poise as your shoulders and neck muscles relax. You'll breathe more freely and move naturally and gracefully. As your self-esteem rises, and the tension leaves your body, you will become less prone to physical problems such as heart disease, poor circulation and cancer.

Your home life will be more rewarding for you and your family, but be warned: at first, you might feel some resistance to your new-found confidence since your family will have learned to deal with the *old* you, and may be unsure how to treat the new. You will have to teach them. If you're more open and self-accepting, they will soon realize that their old way of handling you is no longer appropriate. They might even feel rather insecure, but don't let them manœuvre you back to your old ways – give them a copy of this book to read so they can make the same progress!

You'll find it easier to give love and receive it from your partner, and your sex life will improve. Being loved and cared for will seem the most natural thing in the world.

Living and sharing an intimate relationship with a person with a poor self-image is hard work. They're always looking for reassurance and you can never do enough to convince them you really love them. If they don't love themselves, they instinctively look to their partners and friends to fulfil their needs, and that is an impossibility. The paradox of love is that you can only receive it if you already have it.

You'll be a better parent, because once you value yourself more highly, you will be able to teach your children to value and honour themselves.

Your relationships outside the home will be more fulfilling too. You'll naturally be drawn to the people you want to know, those who share your ideals and have found success in a mutual field of interest. You will treat them with all the respect and warmth you would wish for yourself, and be able to applaud their achievements since you won't perceive them as a threat. Your high self-esteem will be the foundation of your ability to get on well with others, enabling you to cope easily with social situations.

Like is drawn to like in social groupings, and just as people from similar cultural backgrounds tend to seek each other out, so do people with similar levels of self-esteem. We all want to feel comfortable with our friends, and one of the most important factors is some degree of compatibility in self-image and confidence.

Were you one of those people who would go to a party and anxiously look round for another lost soul to talk to? Or avoid anyone who threatened to intimidate you? Perhaps you used to avoid over-assertive people, feeling swept aside by their confident manner, but now they won't bother you in the least. You'll know you have as much to offer as anyone else and will have no hesitation in joining the liveliest group in the room – if that is what you wish. You'll enjoy a good joke, spot the humour in any situation and share your own special sense of fun with those around you.

The way you communicate with other people will be transformed in the space of a few months. You'll be more open and more prepared to show your vulnerability, willing to share your feelings with others, and more comfortable and receptive when they share theirs with you. This is the basis of real intimacy, and genuine long-lasting relationships that enrich and satisfy both parties. You'll enjoy giving and receiving compliments, show your appreciation of others in a sincere way and happily express your warmth and affection.

You'll be able to talk honestly about your accomplishments or shortcomings. You won't feel the need to boast about your achievements or pretend you never make mistakes. You'll accept and give constructive criticism without feeling threatened or wishing to intimidate. You'll realize that even your 'failures' are valuable learning experiences on the way to long-term happiness and success, and not an indicator of loss of face and a lowering of self-esteem.

You won't feel intimidated by others who have more money, status, power, beauty or intelligence than you. A person with lots of money is simply that – a person with lots of money – no better or worse than you. With your new-found confidence, you'll realize that you have everything you need to join the ranks of the wealthy, should you wish.

You'll be more excited by challenges, and more motivated to make the effort to reap the rewards. You'll function better at work than ever before. The restrictions which your low self-esteem used to impose on you will be lifted and you'll want to progress to match your level of ability. You'll know how to handle belligerence and sidestep put-downs. You'll be quick to stand your ground when necessary, but you'll also be able to recognize when it's better to ignore destructive remarks. You won't be drawn into meaningless rivalry or one-upmanship.

You'll achieve more and discover new ambitions, and have the confidence to go for them. Problems will become challenges, and you will rise to overcome them. Conflict, crises and tough times will be seen as part of life to be dealt with firmly and triumphantly. You'll discover greater resources within yourself, just waiting to be tapped.

You'll be able to handle stress with greater ease, manage anxiety and insecurity and allow depression to slip away. You will maintain a spirit of dignity and cheerfulness in difficult times, becoming centred and whole in the face of adversity.

High self-esteem will make all the difference to your future. The time and effort spent working on it is the best investment you will ever make. You'll be inspired to follow your dreams, confident that you can make them come true, and, in the words of Henry David Thoreau, 'live the kind of life you have imagined and come across a success undreamt of in common hours.'

Appendix: The Dynamic Living Institute

The Dynamic Living Institute was founded by Rex Johnson, David Swindley, Joanne Figov and Colleen Johnson to help people transform their lives, achieve health, happiness and success, and learn to access and release the power within to live the kind of lives they want.

Why 'Dynamic Living'? 'Dynamic' means 'activity'. We therefore teach ways of improving your life by taking action, and especially by making the best use of your most important resource – your mind.

We have studied and researched this for nearly twenty years, distilling and integrating the techniques of the best brains in the field. To this we have added and incorporated our own experience in holistic health, education, business, hypnotherapy and psychotherapy.

In addition to writing books and pamphlets, we have made a series of cassette tapes covering all aspects of intelligent, conscious and Dynamic Living, including intuition and mindpower, positive thinking, realizing your dreams, stress management, success and prosperity, dynamic health and attitudinal healing. We also give talks and seminars wherever and whenever we can, and offer individual counselling.

For our free brochure and catalogue, send a stamped addressed envelope to:

The Dynamic Living Institute
45A Branksome Wood Road
Bournemouth   BH4 9JT
United Kingdom

or telephone 0202–762202 or 0202–546145 for further information.

Further Reading

Dyer, Dr Wayne. *Pulling Your Own Strings*, Arrow Books, 1988.

Dyer, Dr Wayne. *Your Erroneous Zones*, Warner, 1992.

Field, Lynda. *Creating Self-Esteem*, Element Books, 1993.

Gawain, Shakti. *Creative Visualisation*, Bantam Books, 1987.

Hay, Louise. *The Power Is Within You*, Eden Grove, 1989.

Hill, Napolean and Stone, W. Clement. *Success Through A Positive Mental Attitude*, Thorsons, 1990.

Jeffers, Susan. *Feel The Fear And Do It Anyway*, Arrow Books, 1991.

McWilliams, John-Roger and Peter. *You Can't Afford The Luxury Of A Negative Thought*, Thorsons, 1990.

Peck, M. Scott. *The Road Less Travelled*, Arrow Books, 1990.

Peiffer, Vera. *Positive Thinking*, Element Books, 1989.

Robbins, Anthony. *Unlimited Power*, Simon and Schuster, 1989.

Index